About the author

Peter Ranis is professor emeritus in political science at the Graduate Center of the City University of New York. His current research interests include the uses of eminent domain on behalf of the working class and cooperative movements in the US, Argentina and Cuba. He has over eighty publications in various fields of social science in such journals as *Monthly Review, Journal of Politics, Studies in Comparative International Development, Desarrollo Economico, Latin American Politics and Society, Labor Studies in Working Class History of the Americas, Socialism and Democracy, Canadian Journal of Development Studies, Current History, Working USA: The Journal of Labor and Society, Situations: Project of the Radical Imagination, Journal of Caribbean Studies, Civilisations, Polity, New Political Science* and *America-at-Work*. He has published four books, among them *Class, Democracy and Labor in Contemporary Argentina* (1995) and *Argentine Workers: Peronism and Contemporary Class Consciousness* (1992).

COOPERATIVES CONFRONT CAPITALISM

CHALLENGING THE NEOLIBERAL ECONOMY

Peter Ranis

Zed Books
London

Cooperatives Confront Capitalism: Challenging the Neoliberal Economy
was first published in 2016 by Zed Books Ltd, The Foundry,
17 Oval Way, London SE11 5RR, UK.

www.zedbooks.net

Copyright © Peter Ranis 2016

The right of Peter Ranis to be identified as the author of this work
has been asserted by him in accordance with the Copyright, Designs and
Patents Act, 1988.

Typeset in Plantin and Kievit by Swales & Willis Ltd, Exeter, Devon
Index by Rohan Bolton
Cover design by Clare Turner

A catalogue record for this book is available from the British Library.

ISBN 978-1-78360-650-4 hb
ISBN 978-1-78360-649-8 pb
ISBN 978-1-78360-651-1 pdf
ISBN 978-1-78360-652-8 epub
ISBN 978-1-78360-653-5 mobi

Printed and bound in Great Britain by
CPI Group (UK) Ltd, Croydon, CR0 4YY

To the courageous Argentine workers recuperating their factories and enterprises as cooperatives and serving as a model for workers everywhere.

CONTENTS

ACKNOWLEDGMENTS

I came to Argentina in 2002, continuing my studies of Peronism and the Argentine working class, my interest since 1963, and the writing of my dissertation on 'Politics, Parties and Peronism: A Study of Post-Perón Political Development' (1965). I returned many times during the administrations of Arturo Illia, Raúl Alfonsín, Carlos Menem and under the Néstor and Cristina Kirchner presidencies. My intention in 2002 was to examine the alternative labor federation, the Central de Trabajadores de la Argentina (CTA). However, shortly after my arrival I was inspired by the dramatic development of the workers' movements to turn failing factories and enterprises into worker cooperatives. That fired my imagination and continues to do so.

Obviously when one writes a book one owes so much to so many. I would be remiss were I not to mention the following friends, compañeros and colleagues who were directly or indirectly involved in my study. Primarily I thank my partner, Jane Necol, who often accompanied me to Argentina and has supported me along the way, offering advice and occasionally correcting a malapropism here and there. I thank my departed friend Fred Wertzer, who read the opening chapter and encouraged me on my way. In Argentina, I want to thank Héctor and Mirta Palomino and Alicia Caplan, who extended their homes and their friendship to me for thirty years, and also my good friend Peloncha Perret, a well-known French chef, whose home served as a restaurant in the Belgrano barrio of Buenos Aires and whom I have known for twenty-five years.

More recently Ramiro Martínez of the Creando Conciencia waste recycling cooperative was vital with his friendship and contacts within the cooperative movements. I was particularly fortunate to have several in-depth interviews with cooperative movement leaders Eduardo Murúa, Luis Caro and Raúl Godoy; and Silvia Díaz and Walter Blanco, La Cacerola cooperative leaders, who deepened my understanding of the various cooperative experiences. My thanks also go to José Hernán Orbaiceta, coordinator and spokesman for INAES (Instituto Nacional de Asociativismo y Economia Social), for clarifying the vast panorama of cooperatives in Argentina. When visiting Neuquén province and the Zanon (Fábrica sin Patrón) worker cooperative, initially in 2006, Mariano Pedrero, legal advisor to the Zanon cooperative, and Professor Fernando Aizicson were very supportive. I also want to thank Silvia Garro and Eduardo Rodriquéz for our many conversations about the worker cooperatives and their interest in my project. Here in New York City, my thanks go to Manny Ness and Chris Michael for suggestions on readings on worker control. Lastly, I want to thank Erik Olin Wright for inviting me to a workshop on 'Empresas Recuperadas' held at the Instituto de Investigaciones Gino Germani at the University of Buenos Aires, October 2015.

I have traveled to Cuba multiple times beginning in 1973 under the auspices of the Center for Cuban Studies and continued to visit the country as a tourist from Puerto Rico in 1978, during the brief opening under President Jimmy Carter, while I was visiting professor at Inter American University at San Germán. I visited Cuba again in the 1980s and then again on a Latin American Studies Association trip in 1999. In my most recent visits, I want to thank the friendship and hospitality of Graciela Morales of COSUDE (Swiss Agency for Development and Cooperation) and Caridad Pacheco González of the Centro de Estudios Martianos. In addition, Pedro Campos has regularly forwarded his informative SPD newsletter after we met in Havana in 2012. Lastly I want to express my appreciation to Cliff DuRand of the Center for Global Justice, based in San Miguel Allende, Mexico, for organizing two stimulating study tours to Cuba in 2012 and 2013.

And finally, my great thanks go as well to the Zed Books and Swales & Willis editors, Dominic Fagan, Kika Sroka-Miller and Caroline Watson, whose genial support was instrumental in the completion of this book.

1 | WHY WORKER COOPERATIVES? THE HISTORICAL UNDERPINNINGS AND DEFENSE OF WORKER COOPERATIVES

Worker cooperatives have captured the mindset and the imagination of countless committed thinkers who have had the working class at the heart of their beings. The grounded basis of their belief systems is that working men and women can labor productively and provide for their families and communities without overlords, captains of industry, magistrates or members of the managerial or ownership classes.

Karl Marx, Eduard Bernstein, Rosa Luxemburg and Antonio Gramsci among many other theorists and political economists – some influentially writing earlier than these notables, others contributing afterwards, all coming from varying ideological principles and orientations – understood the need to confront and supersede the exploitative wage system under existing capitalist relations. It is the wage system that, after all, is at the bottom of how capital continues to achieve profits while immiserating the bulk of the working class. We need to examine the hierarchical relationship between the capitalist and the worker by reenergizing our notion of what is done with capital and by whom. Whether Marxists, neo-Marxists, utopian socialists, reformed socialists, left-liberals, they all recognized the intrinsic value and important interjection of cooperatives as a counterweight to capital–worker societal relationships. Cooperatives offered a major departure from hierarchy at work and working-class exploitation.

Marx, in *Capital*, vol. I, was the most notable, though not the earliest, theorist to note that workers lacked a sense of community and their aggregate social labor is manifested only at the point of exchange when commodities are purchased (Marx 1967a: 73–75). In reality the total collective labor of separate production units represents a dual narrative: workers producing as a group of individuals and workers as part of a society's achieved surplus value produced and exchanged. The product doesn't have much meaning for the worker until it is successfully accepted in the market. Any worker acknowledgement with each other only found confirmation in the sale of the product. Finally, the whole process ends for the worker at that point. Nor, of course, does the worker control what is being produced in the first place. The worker's product is bought by other workers and they, in turn, buy another product with their earnings produced by another worker producing elsewhere. It is this exchange of commodities that Marx envisioned as the lifeblood of capitalism (ibid.: ch. 3). And this exchange is critical for, as Marx noted, 'Circulation sweats money from every pore' (ibid.: 113).

Marx's keen insight was that this was a historical phase of economic development and need not be eternal. Nature has not produced forever one small group of owners and a much larger group of people possessing nothing but their labor power (ibid.: 169). Whatever Marx's critique of worker cooperatives as not spelling the end of capitalism, his many comments about the lack of worker control over what, how and for whom something is produced under capitalism make it clear that he would see cooperatives as enhancing workers' lives while presaging a supersession of this mode of production. In the *Grundrisse*, he clearly sees that capital needs labor, but also that labor needs capital to be productive. It is fully a question of who rules and manages the productive process and for what ends (Marx 1973: 293–310).

It is not by accident that Marx devoted a whole chapter to 'Cooperation' in *Capital*, vol. I. He knew the power of capital and that of labor itself increased multifold in the process of workers working together and producing what an individual worker could not. In fact it this togetherness among workers that greatly enhances their creative and productive powers manyfold (Marx 1967a: ch. 13). Marx said it best when he, speaking of cooperative labor, wrote, '… it excites emulation between individuals and raises their animal spirits … This power is due to cooperation itself. When the laborer cooperates systematically with others, he strips off the fetters of his individuality, and develops the capabilities of his species' (ibid: 329). Of course, it is the capitalist and his managers who takes advantage of worker cooperation. But it need not be because, unquestionably, the capitalist is dispensable in this scenario. Marx wrote in *Capital*, vol. 3,

Cooperative factories furnish proof that the capitalist has become no less redundant as a functionary ... Inasmuch as the capitalist's work does not originate in the purely capitalist process of production, and hence does not cease on its own when capital ceases; inasmuch as it does not confine itself solely to the function of exploiting the labor of others; inasmuch as it therefore originates from the social form of the labor-process, from combination and cooperation of many in pursuance of common result, it is just as independent of capital as that form itself as soon as it has burst its capitalistic shell ... In a cooperative factory the antagonistic nature of the labor of supervision disappears, because the manager is paid by the laborers instead of representing capital counterposed to them. (Marx 1967c: 387)

Marx later adds,

The antithesis between capital and labor is overcome within them, if at first only by way of making the associated laborers into their own capitalist, i.e., by enabling them to use the means of production for the employment of their own labor. They show how a new mode of production naturally grows out of an old one, when the development of the material forces of production and of the corresponding forms of social production have reached a particular stage. (Ibid.: 440)

Nor is it either natural or God-given that the owner/manager be the organizer of men working and producing cooperatively, nor that it be the fixed form of organized production or relationship among workers. Marx wrote in *Grundrisse*, 'The *transformation of labor* (as living, purposive activity) into *capital* is *in itself*, the result of the exchange between capital and labor, in so far as it gives the capitalist the title of ownership to the product of labor (and command over the same)' (Marx 1973: 308).

In 1859, Karl Marx, in *A Contribution to the Critique of Political Economy*, wrote of new modes of production developing within old forms: 'At a certain stage of development, the material productive forces of society come into conflict with the existing relations of production or with the property relations within the framework of which they have operated hitherto. From forms of development of the productive forces these relations turn into their fetters' (Tucker 1978: 4–5). Cooperatives by their organization of the workplace spotlight that inherent capitalist constriction of productive collective labor for collective ends.

And, in *Capital*, vol. 1, when Marx discusses the labor theory of value, he makes clear that it is labor exploitation that is the necessary ingredient of achieving surplus value. Otherwise we are just talking about money remaining constant in the hands of the capitalist. It is the combination of available labor contracted for certain number of hours per day that allows capitalism to 'spring to life' (Marx 1967a: 170). He makes the ironic comment that the worker is even advancing capital to the capitalist by the week or month by receiving wages after his production cycle is done (ibid.: 174). This fact alone demonstrates that the worker is providing his labor power to the capitalist and that, given the ongoing exploitative relationship, he can withdraw that labor power that belongs to him alone.

Marx knew so well that production and exchange are socially constructed and need not be characterized by individualized producing and consuming. In *Grundrisse*, he argued rather that

> The social character of production is presupposed and
> participation in the world of products, in consumption, is not
> mediated by the exchange of mutually independent laborers or
> products of labor. It is mediated, rather, by the social conditions
> of production within which the individual is active … the
> producers change, too, in that they bring out new qualities
> in themselves, develop themselves in production, transform
> themselves, develop new powers and ideas, new modes of
> intercourse, new needs and new language. (Marx 1973: 172, 494)

Marx bemoaned the workers' loss of craft and personality as the industrial revolution deepened as 'labor loses all the characteristics of art, as its particular skill becomes something more and more abstract and irrelevant, and as it becomes more and more a *purely abstract activity*, a purely mechanical activity, hence indifferent to its particular form; a merely *formal* activity, or, what is the same, a merely *material* activity, activity pure and simple, regardless of its form' (ibid.: 297).

Marx went on in the *Grundrisse* to reveal one of the most basic of the capitalist's capacities to magically separate the worker from not only the fruits of his/her labor but the very notion that the worker is the very source and creator of that wealth.

> While capital thus appears as the product of labor, so does the product of labor, likewise appear as capital – no longer as a simple product, nor as an exchangeable commodity, but as *capital*; objectified labor as mastery, command over living labor. The product of labor appears as *alien property*, as a mode of existence confronting living labor as independent, as *value* in its being for itself; the product of labor, objectified labor, has been endowed by living labor as an *alien* power; ... because the whole of real wealth, the world of real value and likewise the real condition of its own realization are posited opposite it as independent existences. As a consequence of the production process, the possibilities resting in living labor's own womb exist outside it as realities – but as *realities alien* to it, which form wealth in opposition to it. (Ibid.: 454)

Nevertheless, despite these horrific and dispirited relationships, workers contained in themselves the potential for rebellion because of their centrality to production, which from time to time they recognized and acted upon. When work stops for whatever reasons, workers recognize it is their labor that makes capital hum and thrive. When mills and factories shut down, capital lies useless waiting for work to begin again. It is at this point that living labor has to recreate itself as independent of objectified labor. In the *Grundrisse*, Marx, with humor and irony, observes these contradictions. He makes the momentous connection that capitalism depends as much on societal domination of a concentrated workforce as on creating the infrastructure for enhancing wealth accumulation.

The Times of November 1857 contains an utterly delightful cry of outrage on the part of a West-Indian plantation owner. This advocate analyses with great moral indignation – as a plea for the re-introduction of Negro slavery – how the free blacks of Jamaica content themselves with producing only what is strictly necessary for their own consumption, and, alongside this 'use value',

regard loafing (indulgence and idleness) as the real luxury good;
how they do not care a damn for the sugar and fixed capital
invested in the plantations, but rather observe the planters'
impending bankruptcy with an ironic grin of malicious pleasure
... They have ceased to be slaves, but not in order to become
wage laborers, but, instead, self-sustaining peasants, working
for their own consumption. As far as they are concerned, capital
does not exist as capital, because autonomous wealth as such
can exist only either on the basis of *direct* forced labor, slavery, or
indirect forced labor, *wage labor*. Wealth confronts direct forced
labor not as capital, but rather as a *relation of domination*. (Ibid.:
325–6)

To thwart these unequal capital/labor relationships, Marx
turned to worker cooperatives as a substantial alternative means of
production. In his *Inaugural Address to the Working Men's International
Association* in London in 1864, Marx made an early assessment of
worker cooperatives. He said,

The value of these great social experiments cannot be over-
rated. By deed, instead of by argument, they have shown that
production on a large scale, and in accord with the behests of
modern science, may be carried on without the existence of a
class of masters employing a class of hands; that to bear fruit, the
means of labor need not be monopolized as a means of dominion
over, and extortion against the laboring man himself; and that,
like slave labor, like serf labor, hired labor is but a transitory
and inferior form destined to disappear before associated labor
plying its toil with a willing hand, ready mind and a joyous heart.
(Tucker 1978: 518)

Though Marx clearly sympathized with cooperative developments,
he saw the attacks by politicians tied to private capital as possibly
insurmountable unless cooperatives 'developed national dimensions,
and consequently to be fostered by national means' (ibid.: 518).

Finally, it was in 1871 that Marx spoke to the International
Working Men's Association only two days after the last resistance
of the Paris Commune had ended. In a mixture of hope and sadness
Marx wrote of the potentiality he saw in working people's abilities

to not only run the Parisian factories but the very centers of French political, administrative and military power (Kamenka 1983: 523ff.). This they demonstrated in the few short weeks of their control over Paris before the onslaught of the overwhelming military force coming out of Versailles. Plans were afoot to restart factories and enterprises abandoned by their owners on a worker-run basis, while associating these cooperatives in one large cooperative union (Tucker 1978: 623).

To appreciate Marx's understanding of the role of cooperatives it is important to know that he was fully aware of the activities and writings of Robert Owen. As recounted by A. L. Morton in *The Life and Ideas of Robert Owen*, Owen was already recognized as a major reforming industrialist with the working class as the key component of British economic development. As Owen wrote, 'Manual labor, properly directed is the source of all wealth and of national prosperity ... Manual labor is of more value to the community than the expense necessary to maintain the laborer in considerable comfort ... that scientific ... aid to man increases his productive powers ... and every addition to scientific or mechanical and chemical power is to increase wealth.' Later Owen wrote 'that the natural standard of value is, in principle, human labor, or the combined manual and mental powers of men called into action' (Morton 1978: 113, 115). Marx was still a young student when he was exposed to the writings and personal commitments of Robert Owen (Marx 1977: 635). Owen's founding of the New Lanark workers' community in England created a self-reliant cooperative village of working men and their families (Morton 1978: 95). He projected a multiplicity of these associated living and working arrangements of between 500 and 3,000 people to eventually become a federation of local communities (ibid.: 45). These visions of collective working-class advancements, which included Owen's belief in the liberating impact on workers of 'eight hours of labor, eight hours of recreation and eight hours of rest,' had important reverberations. This focus on recreation and rest humanizing the worker conforms very closely to Marx's writings in the *Economic and Philosophical Manuscripts* (Fromm 1961: 98–9, 143–4, 168). Owen's focus on a ten-hour workday, the evils of child labor and the importance of children's education are all seen by Marx as necessary preconditions to liberating people's lives (Morton 1978: 123–6; Marx 1967a: 209). Moreover, Owen's assessment of the unnecessary middlemen between producers and the consumers (Morton 1978: 44) becomes a major focus of cooperative development in nineteenth-century England and a notion that Marx understood and accepted in his affirmation of working-class capacity for emancipation. Friedrich Engels, especially in *Socialism: Utopian and Scientific*, lauded Owen's New Lanark experiment by relating that 'when a crisis in cotton stopped work for four months, his workers received their full wages all the time. And with all this the business more than doubled in value, and to the last yielded large profits to its proprietors.' The answer was clear: the capitalist proprietors who previously had taken the bulk of the profits were absent. Engels wrote, 'The newly created gigantic productive forces, hitherto used only to enrich individuals and to enslave the masses, offered to Owen the foundations for a reconstruction of society; they were destined, as the common property of all, to be worked for the common good of all' (Tucker 1978: 691–3).

Though paternalistic in his founding of Lanark and other associated village living arrangements for usually 1,500 people, Owen had sufficient confidence that experience and training of the working class would lead to worker autonomy and efficacy (Morton 1978: 24–5). Though Owen did not accept the need to win control of the state by class struggle, he provided a potential model of a society run by socialist principles based on cooperation and not competition (ibid.: 56, 68).

Yet as advisor to the budding British trade union movement in the early 1830s, Owen wrote (reminiscent of Marx's later appeals to the 'workers of the world unite, you have nothing to lose but your chains'):

We will exhibit to the world ... how easily the most valuable wealth may be produced in superfluity beyond the wants of the population of all countries; also how beneficially, for the Producing Classes ... the present artificial, inaccurate and therefore injurious circulating medium of the exchange of our riches, may be superseded by an equitable, and therefore rational representation of real wealth, and as a consequence ... the causes which generate the bad passions and all the vices and corruptions attributed to human nature, shall gradually diminish until they all die a natural death ... and thus by contrast be

the cause of everlasting rejoicing ... We shall ... remove the
causes of individual and national competition, of individual and
national contests, jealousies and wars, and enable all to discover
their true individual interest and thereby establish peace, good
will and harmony ... (Ibid.: 193–4)

Perhaps the most radical philosophical and political economy
outlook of the day came from William Thompson's *Labour Restored*
(1827). His writings were also known to Marx (Marx 1967a: 361;
Marx 1967b: 322–24). A contemporary of Owen, Thompson
saw things differently and placed greater hopes and aspirations in
workers achieving their goals by their own powers of collective
action, without necessarily depending on paternal benefactors as
Owen believed.

Thompson's outlook and orientation were complex since he
combined theory with prescriptive detail on how workers (he called
them the *industrious class*) could apply capital to working-class
achievements. He saw the capitalist class as a class dependent on the
state and the military to maintain their dominance over the working
class.

Thompson wrote, 'As if it were not enough for the Idle Classes
[capitalists] in their stupid warfare against the Industrious [workers],
to be at once the lawmakers, law-dispensers, and law-executors,
they or their idle associates are almost always *parties* against the
Industrious Classes' (Thompson 2012 [1837]: 5).

Thompson observed that the competitive capitalist system
of Great Britain in the early nineteenth century was thoroughly
skewed against the interests and potential of the working class. He
believed that workers needed to opt out of the competition and
ally together to promote their collective interests, since if workers
competed against each other they were only sustaining the system
that oppresses them. Thompson observed that the so-called 'free
competition' contained legal and institutional restrictions on the
working class, diminishing almost totally their freedom of action,
means of acquiring skills, and access to materials for production
and rights to organize as associations of workers (ibid.: 7). He saw
as unfair a system between labor without capital on the one hand
and capital commanding and enjoying the products of labor on the
other (ibid.: 8). In fact most laborers, as the Industrial Revolution

deepened, still could not consume most of what they produced (ibid.: 9). Laborers necessarily needed to control capital, which required them to 'regulate their labor on a large united scale, before they could do more than dream of enjoying the whole products of their labor ... they must also acquire *power* of the social machine in their own hands, in order to render their knowledge available on a national scale' (ibid.: 15).

In words reminiscent, again, of Marx's *Economic and Philosophical Manuscripts* written two decades later, Thompson wrote,

> [via mutual cooperation the workers] through their own
> mode of exertion ... derive pure pleasures of the senses ... the
> pleasures of muscular and intellectual exertion ... the pleasures
> of sympathy, of the aspect of surrounding smiles and happiness
> including all social pleasures ... mutual esteem formed by the
> industrious themselves and directed solely to the increase of their
> happiness. (Ibid.: 12)

In elegant language, Thompson gave his *cri de coeur*:

> Men and Women of the Industrious Classes! Would you wish
> henceforth to labor not from the pressure or the fear of daily
> want but from the assured hope of varied and unmingled
> enjoyments? Would you wish that your hours of daily labor
> should be reduced to such as are compatible with health
> and length of life? Would you wish utterly to avoid such
> occupations as necessarily engender in a few years peculiar
> disorders incident to each, or to practice them for such a
> limited time only as would avert their mischievous effects on
> the human frame? Would you wish to have a portion of every
> day at your own disposal for intellectual or social pursuits?
> Would you wish, not only to be raised above the fear of want,
> but to possess and enjoy all those articles of food, clothing and
> furniture, the pleasures to be derived from which would more
> than counterbalance the trouble of producing them? Would
> you wish to possess the whole produce of your labor, taxation
> excepted, not only in the particular article fabricated by your
> own hands, but in every other article that your fellow laborers
> produce? (Ibid.: 30)

He believed the working class had the potential to learn and apply their knowledge through 'Communities of Mutual Cooperation' that could become islands of productivity and sustenance. They could do this by contributing a pound or two monthly into a newly formed cooperative association and thus aggregate the finances to create their own means of production. Workers could create capital out of workers' savings as opposed to savings out of profits, the capitalists' methodology. This would free the workers from the capitalist markets, exchanges and exploitative wages which required from the workers 'isolated exertion and individual competition' (ibid.: 28).

Thompson felt that workers had to rid themselves of the notion that human nature required competition to achieve their common needs. He argued that the capitalists had achieved their economic success only by way of the advantages of birth, chicanery and access (ibid.: 22). The workers could then, as Thompson wrote,

In spite of force, fraud and the obstacles of competition, the most usual knowledge, that of themselves and of social arrangements, will speedily pervade the industrious classes: they will learn by means of mutual cooperation of large numbers, supplying each other's most indispensable wants, cultivating equally the peculiar talents and skill of all, to secure to themselves the whole products of their labor. (Ibid.: 29)

He added,

the existing system of force, fraud and competition, differently modified on every spot of the globe, *do not wish* that labor should possess the whole products of its exertions, that they themselves, whether under the name of capitalists, privileged classes, economists, poets, players, or public instructors, are the most insatiable candidates for the prizes of unequal distribution ... and that it is necessary for human welfare to reunite capital and labor, to render all the industrious *capitalist laborers*, laborers possessing all the materials and implements necessary to render their labor productive. (Ibid.: 33)

Another contemporary of Owen, John Francis Bray, whose ideas were also known to Marx, was certainly as dedicated to revolutionary change as Thompson and Marx would be later. Both Thompson and Bray were recently thoughtfully brought to light by Peter Davis and Martin Parker (2007). Bray clearly advocated a change in the social system as opposed to mere governmental changes both in Great Britain and in the US. In terms of reformist governmental approach to working class needs he saw no difference between monarchical England and republican America. He tellingly wrote in *Labor's Wrongs and Labor's Remedies*,

> It must never be forgotten by the working class, when reviewing their wrongs and devising remedies, that their warfare is not against men, but against a system – that they are fighting not against capitalists, as individuals, nor against capital itself, but *against the present mode of applying capital – against that system which gives to irresponsible individuals the power of grinding masses of labor between masses of capital.* There is no remedy for this, except a change of system. Without such a change, the cause of the redemption of the working class is a hopeless one. (Bray 1839: 102)

Bray believed that the working class has to understand that it need not be subordinate to the owner class. Their dependent position is merely because the capitalist class has a monopoly over capital formation supported by the state. This need not be so in perpetuity. As Bray eloquently wrote,

> Thus situated – thus placed, by their position, at the mercy of men and classes who can have no fellow feeling with them – it behooves the producers to determine whether their present condition may not be improved, and to discover what are the particular means whereby such improvement may be effected. The experience of every year and every day teaches them, that, however circumscribed may be their knowledge of the causes which have led to the existing state of things, they cannot know less than those who have hitherto professed to govern and direct them. The time for blind submission to established authorities and usages is passing away …
>
> If the productive classes would be successful in their search for a remedy, they must proceed in the path of discovery unfettered

by those notions which are so sedulously instilled into them, respecting their own inferiority and the eternity of existing usages. As men, and apart from present position as a poor governed class, oppressed by the rich governing class, the producers have nothing to do with the alleged sacredness of established institutions: they have merely to determine whether it be not possible to change *that social whole which keeps them poor*, as well as that governmental part which opposed them because they are poor. (Ibid.: v–vi)

For Bray, men working together would provide that alternative. Workers uniting and buying out the means of production is a real alternative. As Bray wrote, '... it is in the power of the working classes, as a body, to set the new system in motion by their own unaided endeavors ... and when once fairly established, it would undermine the present system in all directions and bring it down in ruins.' And this, Bray argued, could be accomplished by a network of cooperative associations (ibid.: 128). As Bray saw it, it was essentially the quality of economic exchanges (poor wages) that kept the worker subordinate and without the wherewithal to accumulate the capital to provide for the creation of multiple interlocking worker communities throughout England, providing work and well-being (ibid.: 96, 103, 130). British unions, though insufficiently combative in Bray's eyes, had nevertheless shown the capacity to raise the startup funds to provide the initial impetus for autonomous worker associations (ibid.: 153, 173).

Under the deepening Industrial Revolution and persistent exploitation of the working class, later writers took up the cooperative cause. In this regard, Eduard Bernstein, though thoroughly taken to task by Rosa Luxemburg for not providing a revolutionary path to socialism, clearly championed the capacity of workers to provide for their own organizations, be they trade unions or cooperatives. He wrote in *The Preconditions of Socialism* (1899), 'Wherever in the country these cooperatives exist, people become accustomed to engage in manufacture, not just for the sake of profit, but in such a fashion that the worker does not have to lay down his manhood at the factory gate but carries himself with that sense of freedom and that civility which the public spirit in a free community based on equal rights breeds' (Bernstein 1993: 135). He indicated that cooperatives

14 | ONE

are not socialism per se, 'but as workers' organizations they have in them enough of the socialist element for them to be developed into valuable and indispensable instruments of socialist emancipation' (ibid.: 179). Without them, he wrote, 'Where the working class does not possess strong economic organizations of its own and has not attained a high degree of mental independence through training in self-governing bodies, the dictatorship of the proletariat means the dictatorship of club orators and literati' (ibid.: 205).

Even Rosa Luxemburg, though considering Bernstein a revisionist, in her 1900 pamphlet *Reform or Revolution*, argues, compatible with Bernstein, that progressive socialization of the means of production created the germs of the future social order while developing the growing organization and class consciousness of the working class (Luxemburg 1970: 11). However, she did not hold out confidence that cooperatives would not become enmeshed in the capitalist market system for their survival. Her major critique focused on consumer cooperatives as such not providing a path to socialism (Hudis and Anderson 2004 160). On the other hand, Luxemburg argued that producer cooperatives, to be truly effective, had to be extended beyond local and national borders, an aim already understood by Owen, Thompson, Bray, Marx and Engels. Vladimir Lenin, with the introduction to the New Economic Policy (NEP) in the Soviet Union, was also supportive of cooperatives as means to alter working-class culture. He argued in 1923, '... There is only one thing we have left to do and that is to make our people so enlightened that they understand all the advantages of everybody participating in the work of cooperatives, and organizing participation ... There are now no other devices needed to advance to socialism' (Lenin 1965: 3).

Antonio Gramsci, perhaps the most important Marxist theorist of the twentieth century, was instrumental in depicting the challenges facing the working class's ability to counter the capitalist cultural dominance in contemporary society. The forces ranged against the majoritarian working class have been indomitable for over two hundred years. The capitalist state has combined its political agency with its penetration of civil society to create what Gramsci called the 'passive revolution' that controls the forces of production and defends private property. Thus Gramsci, in his *Prison Notebooks*, advocates that the subaltern working class must come up with a 'philosophy of praxis' to contend for power (Gramsci 1971: 106–20; Buttigieg 2005). The key to capitalist success has been in the channeling of working-class grievances into economic ones, bypassing the capturing of the state and creating a counter-hegemony.

Gramsci's notion of passive revolution provides us with insight into capitalism's capacity to prevent the working class from building a counter-hegemonic project as it relegates workers to contesting over economic needs. In this conjuncture, worker cooperatives provide a movement that can escape this subordination and begin a revival of working-class cultural and political emergence. Gramsci, quite rightly, focuses on Marx's understanding of the continuing prominence of the ideological superstructure under capitalism, even when the economic conditions of production have changed. This requires a working-class movement that moves beyond wages, hours and working conditions and into the realm of owning and maintaining production that leads to controlling local economies that demonstrate working-class capacity for impacting on societal economies and, by extension, politics and the concomitant public policy. Cooperatives, indeed, would be the key ingredient to a proletarian hegemonic outcome.

From Gramsci's *Notebooks*, we can see his acute understanding that it will be in civil society that workers will have to assert their rights and capacities to economic and political leadership (Gramsci 1971: 5–23, 201–2). As Peter Thomas argues,

[the passive revolution] involves conscious, political choices: on the one hand, the choice of the ruling classes to develop strategies to disaggregate those working classes and confine them to an economic-corporative level within the existing society, within determinate regimes of accumulation; on the other, the political choices of the subaltern classes that had resulted in a failure to elaborate their own hegemonic apparatuses capable of resisting the absorptive logic of the passive revolution. In other words, the working classes – for different reasons in different countries, but with the same result – had not yet been able to socialize the ideological forms that corresponded to their own experiences of the conflicts within the economic structure of bourgeois society and thus lay the foundations for transforming it. (Thomas 2010: 156–7)

What worker cooperatives provide is a counter-narrative to the one that assumes that only owners and managers can provide leadership and function effectively in the world of production.

Finally, for Eric Hobsbawm, cooperatives, such as those created by Robert Owen, represented 'socialism; or rather the socialism which gained working-class support, even in the 1860s, one which envisaged independent groups of producers without capitalists but supplied by society with enough capital to make them viable, protected and encouraged by public authority but in turn with collective duties to the public' (Hobsbawm 2011: 46). He argues that Gramsci would see institutions like cooperatives as forming collective habits which make social behavior automatic and give the working class, the hitherto subaltern class, the belief in itself as becoming the bearers of a new hegemony (ibid.: 322, 324).

Marx and the other societal critics, as we have seen, understood that cooperatives represented the emancipatory germ that can counter capitalist monopoly over the means of production and societal hegemony. What is needed is to override the nexus of the state with capitalist interests. Development of cooperatives could thrive with a minimum of support from the state's insertion on their behalf, which would allow cooperatives to demonstrate their sustainability and long-term viability.

Thus the visionary ideas of the forbearers and defenders of cooperatives as meaningful ways to explain and achieve worker emancipation must continue to be honed by critical support as we move deeper into the twenty-first century. In the following chapters, we will examine the forms of capital monopolization of the means of production and the continuing struggles of that principal engine – the working class.

2 | THE ROLE OF THE STATE AND THE
US SOCIAL ECONOMY

In the continuing struggle for working-class cooperative formation in the twenty-first century new strategies need to be entertained. Working-class members functioning successfully within cooperatives in multiple societal settings have occurred frequently and continue to be an option. However, as occurred in nineteenth-century England, the success rate is often fraught with uncertainty and failure because cooperatives have often produced and marketed their products within isolated societal silos.

There is little doubt that the future of cooperative formation will need the intervention of public policy under the aegis of a strong state that understands the *raison d'être* of its intervention on behalf of the working class. In that regard the German legal theorist and philosopher Carl Schmitt offers one of the most frontal assaults on an indecisive state. We won't detain ourselves with his later unfortunate support of Hitler's emergency powers but focus on his useful writings between 1922 and 1927. In his two principal works, *Political Ideology* and *The Concept of the Political,* his critique of the vacillating state penetrated by private property and other economic interests is thought-provoking (Schmitt 2005, 2007). He confronted pluralism and its connections to societal moneyed interests. Schmitt sought the independence and autonomy of the political above the politics of everyday life dominated by powerful civil society interests. As he argued, 'The systematic theory of liberalism concerns almost solely the internal struggle against the power of the state. For the purpose of protecting individual freedom and private property, liberalism provides a series of methods for hindering and controlling the state's and government's power' (Schmitt 2007: 70).

The major challenge to the proliferation of cooperatives today is the retreat of the role of state in its responsibilities for establishing societal justice and economic fairness. The struggle today centers on working-class activism combined with the recuperation of state responsibility for employment. We are surrounded by evidence of growing household poverty, unemployment, increasing unprotected informal labor and stagnant wage levels. Between 1948 and 2013, worker productivity in the US increased by almost 250 percent whereas hourly worker compensation increased by only a little over 100 percent. Significantly, productivity and wages grew in lockstep until the mid-1970s when this extreme breach began (Porter 2015). The so-called middle class (read working class) has consistently shrunk in this last half-century with incomes of married couples with children representing the steepest decline (Searcy and Gebeloff 2015). Wages for the workers in the lowest fifth and second-lowest fifth declined by 5.7 and 4.7 percent between 2009 and 2014 (Schwartz 2015). Between the mid-1960s and the late 1970s, the top 1 percent of North Americans earned 8 percent of national income. By 2014 the top 1 percent earned close to 25 percent of national income (Carpenter 2015) and earnings of the top quarter of 1 percent rose 96 percent from 1981 to 2013, while for the highest-paid people in companies employing 10,000 people overall pay jumped 140 percent versus a 5 percent drop for their typical employee (Schwartz 2016). The hidden economic malaise in the US is the increasing numbers of workers that are underemployed and looking for full-time jobs combined with those who are unemployed. These combined figures now have now approached 15 percent (New York Times 2015). Walmart workers exemplify this condition of their absolute inability to survive on less than a forty-hour work week (Reuters 2015a). Much of the hiring that occurs has been concentrated in the low-wage service sectors such as retailing, home healthcare and food preparation, and in other contingent jobs at temporary hiring agencies. These are particularly in job areas that cannot be outsourced and where the creation of community-based cooperatives could well make an important contribution to economic growth and well-being. Cooperatives provide the ideological context to maintain productivity within job settings that defend against worker turnover and decline in morale.

The greatest challenge within capitalist-state arrangements are the myths and fallacies surrounding the role of government, its capacity for engineering change and its potential for fiscal and monetary interventions. The fear of inflation, the fear of unbalanced budgets and the fear of deficit spending are all hobgoblins that provide and maintain governmental options within a rigid framework, an anathema to working-class interests and survival as a productive social class within society. Counter-cyclical governmental interventions of the type that John Maynard Keynes advocated are in retreat. Symbolic of this retreat is the neoclassical acceptance given to the flawed research of economists Kenneth Rogoff and Carmen Reinhart, who argued that economic growth declines dramatically when the public debt threshold exceeds 90 percent of gross domestic product (Krugman 2013).

Robert Skidelsky argues in *Keynes: The Return of the Master* that the Bretton Woods Keynesian economic years in the United States of 1951–73 surpassed the Washington Consensus periods in terms of GDP growth rates, absence of recessions, lower unemployment, and more income equality. In contradiction to neoclassical economists in the US, he demonstrates that despite the better growth rates, lower unemployment and greater income equality, inflation rates were no different in these two periods (Skidelsky 2009: 116–26). Moreover, the United States economy grew more quickly during the 1950s and 1960s despite higher top tax rates (as high as 91 percent).

The state retreat from infrastructure investment, public education, childcare, employment programs, what Fred Block in *The Vampire State* called 'productive consumption,' is seen as fiscally irresponsible. As Block clearly assesses this ongoing conundrum,

> The simple reality is that global financial integration does not work. The pressures of the financial markets operate to keep nations from moving close to full use of their supplies of capital equipment and labor, and there is absolutely no countervailing mechanism that pushes toward full employment because governments have lost most of their ability to pursue fiscal and monetary policies. The dictatorship of international financial markets has become a powerful obstacle to conscious adaptation and effective steering. (Block 1996: 207)

As one antidote to this malaise, Block writes of decentralization and debureaucratization allowing workers to collectively demonstrate their creativity and problem-solving capacities at the firm level unresponsive to capitalist equity firms and their profit-maximization outlooks. He calls this 'popular entrepreneurialism' and advocates the development of cooperatives as one such outlet (ibid.: 257–65).

Samir Amin, in *The Implosion of Contemporary Capitalism*, argues that the financialization of capitalism is due mainly to the subjugation of the management of firms to the principle of shareholder value (Amin 2013: 16). He advocates for the 'gradual conquest of responsibility by workers in the management of their society at all levels – company, local and national' (ibid.: 85) by 'expropriating the facilities of runaway companies in favor of their workers and local governments' (ibid.: 101) and 'socializing the management of nationalized monopolies' (ibid.: 127).

In *The Predator State: How Conservatives Abandoned the Free Market and Why Liberals Should Too*, James K. Galbraith presents a very sharp assessment of a United States government as a state that has the potential to intervene for the public good on behalf of workers and consumers, as in the days of the New Deal, but instead has been captured by corporate interests that have colonized it on their behalf. Using the bromides of monetarism, supply-side economics, tax cuts and deregulation, the government has derogated its responsibilities on behalf of the needy, while it has become a reliable surrogate for corporate interests. Galbraith calls this the Predator State. He writes,

> It is a coalition of relentless opponents of the regulatory framework on which public purpose depends, with enterprises whose major lines of business compete with or encroach on the principal public functions of the enduring New Deal. It is a coalition, in other words, that seeks to control the state partly in order to prevent the assertion of public purpose and partly to poach on the lines of activity that past public purpose has established. They are firms that have no loyalty to any country. They operate as a rule on a transnational basis, and naturally come to view the goals and objectives of each society in which they work as just another set of business conditions, more or less inimical to the free pursuit of profit. (Galbraith 2008: 131)

Galbraith continues his indictment.

> These developments – the placement of corporate men in charge of the state on the one hand, and the decline in their base of popular support on the other – have a profound effect on the

character of the state itself. They bring on a tendency to run the state as though it were, in fact, just a corporation, with the rules that govern companies displacing the rules that govern republics. And so today we live in a *corporate republic*, where the methods, norms, culture, and corruption of government have become those of the corporation. (Ibid.: 144)

He continues, 'Everywhere you look regulatory functions have been turned over to lobbyists. Everywhere you look, public decisions yield gains to specific private persons. Everywhere you look, the public decision is made by the agent of a private party for the purpose of delivering private gain. This is not an accident; it is a system' (ibid.: 147).

Jacques Rancière, in *Dissensus: On Politics and Aesthetics*, encapsulates this struggle in a capitalist democratic state between defending primarily a select set of principles and constituencies and bypassing and ignoring the rest. That is, that

> democracy as a form of government is threatened by democracy
> as a form of social and political life and so the former must
> repress the latter … citizenship means the rule of equality
> among people … that is, as private individuals subordinate to
> the power of ownership and social domination … from whose
> scope many categories of people are excluded and which
> limits citizens by placing certain problems out of their reach
> … Democracy cannot be reduced to the universal power of
> the law against the particularity of interests, because it is the
> very logic of the police to carry out a continuous privatization
> of the universal … The universal has to be supplemented
> by subjectivation that stymies the relentless privatization
> of public life … Over the last 30 years, both the soft name
> of modernization and the candid name of neo-conservative
> revolution have been used to effect a *reversal* of the democratic
> process that had broadened the public sphere by turning
> matters of private life – such as work, health and pensions
> – into public concerns related to equal citizenship … Such an
> inscription is made by subjects who are newcomers, who allow
> new objects to appear as common concerns, and new voices to
> appear and to be heard. (Rancière 2013: 47, 56–7, 60)

Partha Chatterjee, in *The Politics of the Governed*, concurs, focusing upon the distance between the values of the large property holders in civil society and the vast majority of people in the community without basic rights and protections. He is largely speaking of India, but his analysis is far more universal. The unorganized working class, the marginalized, and the unemployed Chatterjee sees as essentially paralegal second-class citizens within political society but hardly legitimized within recognized civil society (Chatterjee 2004: 41). As he argues,

> Property is the conceptual name of the regulation by law of relations between individuals in civil society. Even where social relations are not, or have never been, molded into the proper forms of civil society, the state must nevertheless maintain the fiction that in the constitution of its sovereignty, all citizens belong to civil society and are, by virtue of that legally constructed fact, equal subjects of the law. Yet in the actual administration of governmental service ... the fictive quality of this legal construct must be recognized and dealt with. (Ibid.: 74)

The United States fits this dichotomy between civil and political society more than most advanced capitalist societies. It is far less egalitarian than the European Community countries and has one of the highest Gini coefficients of inequality, comparable to many of the poorest, most stratified societies (Stiglitz 2012: 23). In 2013 the US Gini index was .476, twice as high as that of most western European countries (Lepore 2015: 26). This inequality in which the top 1 percent receives 20 percent of national income skews consumption at the lower ends of the economic spectrum, among those who would consume most of their earnings and thus boost the national economy and growth rates (Stiglitz 2012: 85). The post-recession crisis has skewed income distribution even more. Between 2009 and 2011 the top 1 per cent of income earners grew by 11.2 percent while incomes of the bottom 99 percent fell by 0.4 percent. The top 1 percent enjoyed 122 percent income gains in the first two years of the recovery from recession (*New York Times*, 4 May 2013). Meanwhile capital gains tax cuts led to speculative booms in the tech and housing bubbles and higher dividend distribution rather than new productive investments. At the same time these developments are surrounded by a deficit fetishism that puts artificial restraints on government investments in public goods, regulating the market and providing social protection (Stiglitz 2012: 172, 236).

Thomas Piketty, in *Capital in the Twenty-First Century*, has also been in the forefront of documenting United States and European income disparities. He emphasizes the Rhenish capitalism of Germany and the Nordic countries, where stakeholders play a role in terms of degrees of shared social ownership, and Anglo-Saxon capitalism dominated by shareholder interests (Piketty 2014: 145). These differences between models of capital accentuate the vast income disparities in the United States.

Piketty shows how the minimum wage in the United States reached its maximum level half a century ago. In 1969, it was $10.10 in 2013 dollars and unemployment was 4 percent. In 2013, for example, the minimum wage in the United States was $7.20, whereas France's minimum wage was over €11 per hour (ibid.: 309). At the upper end of the economic spectrum we see that the number of those making more than $1 million a year virtually explodes in the same period (ibid.: 314). Income disparity in the United States is accentuated by the rise of 'super managers', particularly in the financial sectors. The result of this is that in 2010 the top 10 percent earned 48 percent of national income (ibid.: 323). Wealth income is even more skewed in the United States, with the top 10 percent owning 70 percent and the top 1 percent capturing close to 35 percent of total wealth (ibid.: 348–9). Social disparities are magnified in the United States by the fact that tax revenues are at 30 percent whereas, for example, France's are 50 percent and Sweden's are 55 percent (ibid.: 475).

Piketty's central thesis is that return on capital is greater than the rate of a country's growth in output and income ($r > g$). As he puts it, 'This inequality expresses a fundamental logical contradiction. The entrepreneur inevitably tends to become a rentier, more and more dominant over those who own nothing but their labor' (ibid.: 571). Piketty acknowledges that new forms of capitalist management and control and shared ownership must be found to inhibit such massive and unfair income and wealth distributions. Of course, these organizations already exist in terms of the growth of worker cooperatives in all the countries that Piketty investigates.

We are increasingly looking at a world where the states are losing absolute control over the uses and applications of technology. In fact states seem to be competing in the world over disciplining the labor forces in their respective countries in order to enhance each country's competitive advantage and to prepare its working classes for further sacrifices and continuous loss of bargaining power with big capital. In a sense each national state seems to be providing the playing field upon which big capital can thrive. The exponential growth of the digital economy, represented by Uber, Airbnb, TaskRabbit and the unequal demographic use of the internet, has served to weaken the social and economic rights of the working class, especially those at the lower end of the sociological spectrum.

Karl Marx was the first who clearly understood that the global lives of the working class were being homogenized with the proliferation of new forms of technology. He wrote of the growing competition among the bourgeoisie the world over, even accentuated during economic crises within capital, to constantly seek to bring down workers' wages. Thus, in Marx's words in *The Communist Manifesto*, 'making their livelihood more and more *precarious*' (Marx, in Tucker 1978: 480).

The environment for such state abandonment of its responsibility for the working class, of course, is first accentuated in the industrial age, and it is there, and particularly in the United States, that unbridled capitalism is given its head. Nowhere is this better described and analyzed than in Harry Braverman's classic book *Labor and Monopoly Capital*, in which he describes the uses and applications of Frederick Taylor's 'Scientific Management' and its technological innovation within the manufacturing setting. He provides the context in which the United States working class departs from any sense of revolutionary confrontation before the initiatives of capitalist workplace reforms and their subsequent adjustment to merely bargaining over their diminishing share of what is produced.

The transformation of capitalist technology and its vast impact on working-class subordination is at the centre of Braverman's thesis and it is clearly still relevant, though its productive core has markedly shifted. Yet it is labor's intelligent adaptability and capacity for innovation that allows capital to produce the conditions that enhance its productivity (Braverman 1974: 56).

As Braverman describes these conditions,

> The spider weaves, the bear fishes, the beaver builds dams and houses, but the human is simultaneously weaver, fisherman,

builder, and a thousand other things combined in a manner which, because this takes place in, and is possible only through, society, soon compels a social division ... and invents standards unknown to any animal but the human species as a whole finds it possible to do this, in part through the social division of labor. (Ibid.: 72)

Thus, as the mode of production passes into the capitalist's hands, the labor process becomes more regulated by external forces alien to the worker herself. As the process develops and deepens, the knowledge of that process becomes more and more the province of the capitalist owners and managers, and only its application and execution are left to the worker (ibid.: 119).

As Braverman writes,

These scientific managers have not ceased to complain bitterly, as is their wont, of the characteristics of a working population which they themselves have shaped to suit their ends, but they have not yet found a way to produce workers who are at one and the same time degraded in their place in the labor process, and also conscientious and proud of their work. (Ibid.: 133)

As the industrial process continues in its complexity,

... the control of humans over the labor process turns into its opposite and becomes the control of the labor process over the mass of humans ... The capacity of humans to control the labor process through machinery is seized upon by management ... as the prime means whereby production may be controlled not by the direct producer but by the owners and representatives of capital. (Ibid.: 193)

The crux of the matter is that

Machinery offers to management the opportunity to do by wholly mechanical means that which it had previously attempted to do by organizational and disciplinary means. The fact that many machines may be paced and controlled according to centralized decisions, and that these controls may thus be in the hands of management, removed from the site of production to the office – these technical possibilities are of just as great interest to management as the fact that the machine multiplies the productivity of labor. (Ibid.: 195)

And, of course, Braverman understands that this breakdown of autonomous work is not limited to the industrial sector but, as capitalism expands and proliferates into the service economy, these controlling procedures expand apace.

Building on Braverman's assessment of working lives under monopoly capital and the resulting loss of worker autonomy and contestation, Ursula Huws, in *Labor in the Digital Economy*, offers an even more stark account of workers in a digital age. The geometric progression of new technologies consumed by all the world's inhabitants to one degree or another has also had devastating impacts on the production cycle. Huws demonstrates with dramatic accounts how Marx's 'reserve army of labor' has become a clearly international phenomenon from which no country, particularly the wealthier nations, is immune (Huws 2014). Digital technology, she argues, has provided the rationale for the enhanced casualization of labor, the subcontracting phenomenon and the downsizing pattern observed in contemporary capitalist development (ibid.: ch. 1).

She argues: 'Once expropriated, the knowledge and experience, or "craft," of these workers can be dispensed with, and cheaper, less skilled workers substituted to operate the new machines or administer the new systems.' As the levels of digital sophistication proceed, 'it is increasingly common for people to switch between public and private sector employment and to be required to exhibit an increasingly convergent range of "skills," "abilities," and "competencies" ranging from use of standard software packages to "being a good team player" or possessing "good time management skills"' (ibid.: 74–5).

Huws makes abundantly clear the new intensity and precariousness of the situation of the contemporary working class. Conspiring against a sense of working-class solidarity is the impact of the digital economy upon workers' sense of collectivity. As individual capitalist enterprises 'define new protocols, performance targets and quality standards … camaraderie, idea sharing, and mutual support may become its victims' (ibid.: 78).

Huws describes the wholesale commodification of the information technology and how it seeps into all forms of production and consumption. No one is immune and all, willingly or not, are part of the value chain that provides big capital with its profit margins (ibid.: ch. 3). Thus, in this competitive environment, the state, or its various subdivisions in the United States, aims to attract domestic and foreign capital and often even aims to reduce the cost of public services by outsourcing them to global suppliers (ibid.: 100). Even in nations like Great Britain and Sweden, which had or have the largest decommodified public sectors, they have been either recommodified in the British case, beginning under Thatcher, or in the Swedish case are the prime targets of recommodification (ibid.: 133). This is the outcome because as the role of information workers grows worldwide owing to the availability of communications technologies, the public sector functions can be increasingly privatized or offshored (ibid.: 138).

Thus it becomes essential for state entities to form strong alliances with their national workforce to provide employment and prevent downsizing and offshoring, so that what remains of welfare capitalism can provide for the nucleus of society to offer a measure of social justice and fair income remuneration. Governments must decide what their priorities are. Unmanageable levels of worker unemployment or the continuation of capital penetration and use of workers as pure commodities? Workers, with their intelligence, judgment, knowhow and skills, need to be encouraged and protected as a national resource and an ethical requirement.

Since Occupy Wall Street in 2011 there has been a clearer understanding on the part of the public at large that income distribution for the working class is skewed. Americans, in their views of worker rights and income inequality, have become notably more cognizant of the societal disparities. In a major survey 61 percent of Americans felt they had no chance to get ahead in society, and over two-thirds felt incomes should be more equitably distributed and that the gap between them and the rich was getting larger. The respondents argued for paid sick leave for employees who are ill (85 percent) and paid leave for parents of new children and employees caring for sick family members (80 percent). Further, the survey reported that 72 percent of respondents argued that chain stores and fast-food outlets should give workers at least two weeks' notice of any changes in their work schedules or provide them with extra pay (*New York Times*, 4 June 2015). These responses pinpoint dramatically what the unorganized working class in the United States faces in their daily struggles at the workplace.

The resourcefulness needed to combat these inequities is no better depicted than by Linda Tirado in her book *Hand to Mouth: Living in Bootstrap America*. She explains in no uncertain terms and in vibrant colors that a readymade class consciousness is certainly available but hard to come by without a modicum of job security. Tirado really lays bare the 'short and simple annals of the working poor.' And it is the working poor that she describes in firsthand accounts of their daily struggles.

Job stability is, of course, a vanishing feature among workers at the bottom of class stratification. Tirado writes,

> Rest is a luxury for the rich. I get up at 6 a.m., go to school (I have a full course load, but I only have to go to two in-person classes), then work, I get the kids, then I pick up my husband, then I have half an hour to change and go to Job 2. I get home from that at around 12:30 a.m., then I have the rest of my classes and work to tend to. I'm in bed by 3. This isn't every day. I have two days off a week from each of my obligations. I use that time to clean the house and … see the kids for longer than an hour and catch up on schoolwork. Those nights I'm in bed by midnight, but if I go to bed too early I won't be able to stay up the other nights because I'll fuck my pattern up, and I drive an hour home from Job 2 so I can't afford to be sleepy. I never get a day off from work unless I am fairly sick. It doesn't leave you much room to think about what you are doing, only to attend to the next thing and the next. Planning isn't in the mix. (Tirado 2014: xiv)

Tirado explains:

> This is my bottom line point about work and poverty. It's far more demoralizing to work and be poor than to be unemployed and poor. I have never minded going without when I wasn't working. It sucks not to be able to find a job, but you expect to be tired and pissed off and to never be able to leave your

house when you're flat broke. Working your balls off, begging for more hours, hustling every penny you can, and still not being able to cover your electric bill with any regularity is soul-killing ... Whenever you are working for the kind of place that has a corporate office, you're typically given the fewest possible hours – definitely less than full-time, because then they'd have to pay you benefits. (Full time is often on the twenty-eight to thirty-two-hours-a-week range, to boot.) But even though your employer might schedule you for twenty hours a week, you might wind up working ten, or thirty. It depends on how busy it is – when it's slow, they send you home, and when it's busy, they expect you to stay late. They also expect you to be able to come in to cover someone's shift if a co-worker gets sick at the last minute. Basically, they're expecting you to work all the time. Scheduling is impossible. (Ibid.: 7, 19)

Tirado explains how easy it is to fire a worker under non-union contracts that make one an at-will employee. That provision allows a worker to be fired for any reason outside of current civil rights legislation, and to contest it would require an impossibly long and expensive legal suit unavailable to the worker. As Tirado writes,

I've been fired because my boss made a mistake on some paperwork. I've been fired because I had the flu. I've been fired because I wouldn't sleep with someone. I've been fired because I did sleep with someone – I resent the fuck out of it every time my schedule's been cut and then I've been called in for tons of extra hours, as though my time weren't worth anything, just so that my boss can be sure not to pay me a minute that I'm not absolutely necessary. I resent signing away my ability to get a second job and being told that I can't work more than twenty-eight hours a week either. (Ibid.: 20, 25–6)

Humiliations on the job abound.

Mostly I make it through a whole day, but sometimes it's just not in the cards. The night before my record-setting morning, I'd made it home from work at ten p.m. and passed out by eleven. I'd been working extra and was short on sleep to begin with. My boss called at five a.m. wanting me to come in. I drank some coffee and dragged my sorry ass out the door, and when I showed up, he was mad that it had taken me half an hour to come in. He'd been under the impression that when I said, 'I'll be there,' I meant that I'd use my teleportation device instead of the beater car I had at the time. I blew if off, figuring that he was just in a bad mood. But he simply couldn't let it go – every time someone complained about this or that setup not being done properly he said that if only I'd been there on time we'd have made it.

I lost it. Completely. This is the version of what I said that I can best remember through my blistering rage: 'If you think I'm so goddamned terrible, why did you call me in? Did you not realize that I'd be on a fourteen-hour shift and that I was running on a few miserable fucking hours of sleep? WHAT IS WRONG WITH YOU, YOU INCOMPETENT FUCKING ASSHOLE?' And I said all this in my outdoor voice. In front of customers. I spent the afternoon looking for work, as I was newly unemployed. (Ibid.: 58–9)

Despite the degradations on the job, short-term workers are always expected to be of good cheer and be happy in their work. And when a fellow worker of an indefatigable, optimistic nature is finally beaten down, Tirado writes, 'it is heart-wrenching to watch that fade, like watching a star die or something. I can't think of anything poetic and tragic enough to describe it' (ibid.: 67).

Tirado explains with insight why workers don't always fit our presupposed notions of what they should care about. She writes,

I do not care about the whales. I'm unfussed about owls. I could give you a lot of reasons why I don't consider myself an environmentalist, but it mostly comes down to this: my issue is people in the micro. Once we've hit the part where my own species is mostly taken care of, I'll start to worry about African rhinos … But I also get why people aren't breaking down the doors of the polling places. For one, we can't keep track of whether we're supposed to bring a DNA sample or a urine sample this time to prove our identity and residency. It keeps changing. For another, the hours and polling location in poorer neighborhoods keep getting cut for some reason ... I tend to think the economic policies aren't going to change much no matter how badly we want them to, but I'm sure that all my friends should be able to get married with whomever they wish, and I like the idea that I can get birth control without having to ask the blessing of the Republican leadership. (Ibid.: 153–6)

Tirado's condition emphasizes how important it is that with the decline of traditional blue-collar proletarian jobs and their union affiliations, new institutions and measures must be found to represent the working class both in the declining industrial sectors and in the growing service and professional sectors (*New York Times*, 20 November 2014). There is a special need today to provide new mobilization tools and procedures to preserve the rights of the working class under neoliberal austerity-driven capitalism.

Tirado's subjugation is embedded in the very nature of working for an employer, whether one negotiates individually, as she does with various bosses, or whether groups of workers bargain collectively by way of a union contract with an employer. The consent that workers give to work is basically a coercive one, since there are no alternatives to working for owners of capital. As David Ellerman sees it, it is a dubious voluntary contract for renting oneself out. The worker, he argues, is used as if he were a tool and there is no alternative but to work for some employer. So it is by no means a voluntary consensual association and the result is, of course, not democratic. As he writes,

The only people who are under the authority of the owners and their agents are the ones who work their property, the employees of the corporation ... But the very idea that employees qua workers (i.e. as those who are governed or managed) would have any standing in that governance seems an outlandish perversion of the very idea of 'ownership'. (Ellerman 2015: 2)

Steven Greenhouse, in *The Big Squeeze: Tough Times for the American Worker*, comments that, symbolic of this malaise, 'American workers are viewed as voters, as NASCAR fans, as Oprah watchers, as Bud drinkers, as potential members of the ownership society, but they are rarely viewed as workers qua workers' (Greenhouse 2008:

303). And often the public at large, composed largely of the working class, is widely misinformed concerning the role and benefits of the public sector in their lives. As Johnson and Kwak write in *White House Burning: Our National Debt and Why It Matters to You*, 'According to a 2008 survey, 44 percent of people who receive Social Security retirement benefits say that they "have not used a government social program." The same goes for 40 percent of Medicare recipients and 43 percent of people who have collected unemployment insurance benefits. Of the people who denied using any government social programs, 94 percent had benefited from at least one' (Johnson and Kwak 2013: 10). As Noam Chomsky writes, 'Support has been so high that in the late Reagan years, more than 70% of the public "thought health care should be a constitutional guarantee," while 40% thought it already was' (Chomsky 2013: 692).

The digital-technological revolution, multinational corporate outsourcing, the growth of the global South's increasingly skilled workforce and worldwide trade and open-market access have put enormous pressure on the United States working class (Carroll 2010). Most dramatically, the US has lost 864,000 non-farm jobs just since 2009 (Moberg 2013).

In conclusion

The picture is as bleak as a Victorian novel depicting England a century and a half ago. It is a scenario that exemplifies clear capitalist cultural domination in contemporary society. From the retrograde minimum wage to the globalization challenge, declining unionism, and increasing educational, health and retirement gaps it is a very dismal picture. The sub-prime mortgage home foreclosure epidemic, the student debt crisis and the credit card debacle have only deepened working-class malaise. What needs to occur is the cultural and political emergence of the working class.

The challenges to working-class resurgence are multiple. The state must not retreat from supporting working-class cooperative initiatives. The state has the power and reach to use its public policy prerogatives to defend the overwhelming majority of its citizens. This is a matter of the highest priority, particularly in the United States. The public good has to be reimagined as a responsibility of good government. Unemployment and poverty need not be the continual residue of market economies. They are, rather, a consequence of retroactive neoliberal shortsightedness and the greed of money managers and administrators. The state has to literally declare its independence from the capitalist class and become the mediator of what is good for both capital and labor, employer and employee. Market economy and democratic politics are too critical to leave in the hands of the capitalist class with its sectarian ideology. They have shown over and over again that their values are not consonant with the needs of US society as a whole.

We need to revisualize work organization, democratic procedures, the capacity for worker self-management, the fostering of community togetherness and the political outreach that can combine to provide an alternative to the hierarchical private corporations that stand front and center in the neoliberal capitalist economy.

Eminent domain, as we will demonstrate, is available to meet America's socio-economic challenges and provide the multiple strata of working classes with the wherewithal to reclaim their dignity, their autonomy and their rights to social and economic justice. Worker cooperatives require the public policy support of eminent domain on behalf of workers for the clear benefit of authentic economic development and the critical defense against unemployment and poverty.

3 | WORKER COOPERATIVES IN THE POST-OCCUPY DIGITAL ECONOMY

The Occupy Wall Street (OWS) movement of 2011 had clearly expressed the hopes and great potentialities of the working class both in the US and globally through words and actions. The 99 percent had spoken up and said that they would no longer do the bidding of the 1 percent. In essence it was the revolt of the masses, the underclasses in their various guises. People in Zuccotti Park in New York City, those in Tahrir Square in Cairo, Madrid, Madison, Wisconsin and elsewhere imagined doing incredible things autonomously and with purpose. They developed islands of political and economic autonomy that drew attention to what people can do on their own and for themselves. From many walks of life they stood up and spoke with measured purpose and were heard. This has been a valuable lesson for the American working class and their right to stand up and prevent their jobs in factories and enterprises from being eliminated.

The OWS was inspirational and provocative but in the last analysis it lacked grounding in the productive agencies of the economy. In its amorphousness it raised all the right questions but the answers needed to be ensconced where workers lived and worked. In that it failed, since its guiding force was essentially rootless intellectual leftists not grounded in the very means of production that needed to be confronted.

The economic crash and recession of 2008 only heightened the concerns that we have about the capacity and willingness of liberal capital to provide justice and equity for the overwhelming majority of Americans. The lack of societal concern on the part of the large hierarchical capitalist firms and financial institutions has never been so clearly manifested. OWS and its successors represented a historically momentous breakthrough that demonstrated the potential for workers, social movements, progressive intellectuals and labor unions to indeed come together at crucial times. It represented a clear cultural break with the normality of capitalist society and promised a future path under the right conditions.

The United Nations declared 2012 the International Year of Cooperatives. This only added to the imperative to explore the many ways that worker-managed factories and enterprises can be an alternative to traditional capitalist firms and companies. However, we speak here of worker cooperatives, not credit unions, utility cooperatives, marketing cooperatives, and ESOPs (Employment Stock Option Plans) and other forms of cooperatives, such as consumer cooperatives, that may be an improvement on oligarchic capital firms, but do not offer the working class control and direction of their work sites. Many ESOPs, for example, are run as tax shelters for owners and managers. At the same time, distributing profit shares to their employees creates marginal wage differentials for them in return for mollifying any potential worker confrontation with their paternalistic job environment. Often, even if well intentioned, ESOPs provide their bosses with labor peace by offering stock incentives to the workers, improving their income and pension payouts without vindicating worker collective rights on the job. In fact one could argue that workers under those conditions become ever more accepting and conditioned to the arbitrary decisions foisted upon them in the workplace. See, for example, the views of Louis Kelso, whose proposals would turn workers into small capitalist employees content with an incremental increase in their takehome pay by virtue of profit shares (Erdal 2011). On the other hand, consumer cooperatives are often not good examples of worker cooperatives because they have clear management controls and are membership organizations that involve holding an identification discount card. An authentic worker cooperative has to go beyond being a provider; it has to involve a democratic organization and a participatory ideology (Benkler 2015).

What we are speaking of is worker cooperatives formed from below by way of occupation, struggle and consciousness of their rights on the part of laborers and employees. These cooperatives as worker-managed enterprises, for a number of institutional and societal reasons, represent alternative productive vehicles attempting to override the impact of deindustrialization, globalization and the neoliberal ideological offensive. The social economy and solidarity relationships represented by worker-managed enterprises need to be examined as focal points for working-class capacities to sustain the possibilities of a productive worker-centered culture. These alternatives have become ever more urgent given the shrinkage of labor union density, especially the decline of private-sector organized workers. Worker-managed factories and enterprises are called for particularly at this moment with the declining industrial base of the American working class. Perhaps upward of 25 percent of the American industrial heartland lies idle with the potential for unemployed workers to create cooperatives and other self-managed enterprises to fill that vacuum. But they need not be limited to laborers. The large bulk of the American working class finds itself in the services, in commerce and as contingent workers, subcontracted workers and immigrant workers. All of these precarious groups of workers deserve the benefits and entitlements that capital-labor reorganization into cooperatives would provide for them. And indeed, in the service and retail sectors, as opposed to the manufacturing sector, we see positive signs of US workers coming together to form cooperatives as alternatives to worker impoverishment and powerlessness. Among cooperative formations there is evidence of positive outcomes in low worker turnover and cooperative longevity compared to private sector firms (Abell 2014: 6-7, 13). Moreover cooperative members tend to earn almost twice as much as in non-cooperative businesses and are much more likely to spend their income within the local economy (Kelly et al. 2016: 17).

We need to operate under new categories of the working class because of the decline of the proletariat at the source of production in the West, leaving the center of value-added production in the hands of the Indian and Chinese subcontinent. There are indications that if new forms of worker organization emerge they will most likely occur in European countries like Italy, France, Germany, the Scandinavian countries, Greece and Spain. The United States has the conditions to substantially complement these developments despite the disheartening situation of contemporary labor struggles.

In terms of point of production and commitment to militant mobilization and openness to new forms of worker engagement, a totally counter-intuitive picture emerged in Argentina. There, the workers most open to radical, militant change were teachers, telephone technicians and bank employees. The less open were metal workers, auto workers and textile workers, and in the middle were electrical workers working for the state power company, Segba, having one foot in the public sector as well as providing a critical input for private industrialization production (Ranis 1992).

What needs to be considered today is an understanding that it is no longer the traditional industrial proletariat that must be engaged but the precariat, made up of a part-time and contingent workforce, a reserve army of labor which is now totally international because of globalization and technology making for more precarious workers each and every day.

Workers need to embrace the knowledge that worker-managed workplaces are a realistic and grounded alternative to economic norms. Certainly, in countries such as Argentina, Italy, Spain, Venezuela, Brazil, Canada, England, France and Greece, worker self-managed experiments have asserted themselves as new and stable forms of worker solidarity, autonomy and participatory initiatives within the capitalist economy. These examples of the twenty-first century's first decade and a half demonstrate that class consciousness and political awakening are enhanced, not diminished, by workers banding together into economic units that depend upon working-class and middle-class workers' initiatives to provide new forms of penetrating the local economies and mediating the challenges of the capitalist marketplace.

This challenge is no more clear than in the exploding digital platform economy, the so-called 'sharing economy.' Since the 2008 recession in the United States newly created groups of the unemployed among better-educated middle-class workers have been searching for viable employment. We are now dealing more and more with workers who are considered independent contractors, some of them middle-class workers, who are exploited, though their social status may separate them from the bulk of the working class. It is estimated that approximately one third of the US workforce are considered independent contractors.

One particular digital platform employer – Uber – exemplifies this pattern. Its managers, in the rhetoric of Walmart's 'associates', call their drivers 'partners.' In February 2016, the New York City and San Francisco Uber drivers filed petitions in the federal courts and with the National Labor Relations Board requesting that they be considered employees. Disputes have broken out in New York City because of unilateral employer policies that have set fares too low for the drivers to make a decent living. Drivers already feel squeezed as they receive no employee benefits and pay their Uber employers 20–25 percent of their earnings as a fee for the service. Additionally, of course, they must buy their own car, maintain it and pay for its upkeep and insurance costs. At the same time, Uber pricing decisions, a no-tipping policy and the ease with which the drivers can be 'deactivated', make it clear they are employees of the gig economy (Feuer 2016).

In fact, within the digital economy middle-class, college-educated workers hire college-educated workers to clean homes (TaskRabbit). Others rent their apartments (Airbnb). The austerity economy finds higher-educated people displacing those workers with only high school education (Schor 2015). In the last analysis all are contingent workers subjected to the whims of the marketplace and playing by the rules of Darwinian venture capitalism.

The US provides a challenging arena for confronting the digital platform economy that provides employment for so many middle-class workers, workers without guaranteed health benefits, pensions, minimum wages, job security, workplace protections and subject to on-the-job surveillance. Developing cooperatives within the digital economy is very viable because human resources are the key (e.g. software engineering) rather than large amounts of money. Cooperatives embody equal levels of worker contributions and high participation in research and development as well as localizing workers in their communities, thus emphasizing a more trusting and reciprocal productive environment (Sundararajan 2015).

Trevor Scholz has argued that regulatory law has not been able to keep up with the technological changes that are giving rise to the 'for profit' sharing economy. Scholz sees the digital 'sharing economy' as a 'shinny sharp tip of a spear of convenience made up of deregulation, union busting, classism and racism.' Christian Fuchs writes of the need to form worker-controlled companies in the digital industries, '… no matter if it disturbs social media, software engineering, the freelance economy … or information and communications technology' (Fuchs 2016: 11). And Scholz advocates for digital cooperatives that provide collective ownership, democratic governance and worker solidarity – a virtual cooperative internet movement as an ethical self-managed counterpart to the capitalist business model (Scholz 2015). Uber drivers would represent a model of a digital cooperative in the various cities where they are a crucial mode of transportation!

For all the above reasons, I use and have used the term 'middle-class workers' pointedly because it is necessary to redefine what we mean by the working classes. It is disturbing to find that the term 'working class' has largely disappeared from the US lexicon. In my research two decades ago interviewing 110 Argentine workers from teachers, telephone technicians, and bank employees to auto workers, electrical workers, metal workers and textile workers I was faced with the need to categorize their disparate and various social background and values (Ranis 1992, 1995). I determined that for many members of the working class I needed to change the term 'middle class' from a compound noun to an adjective so as to more clearly describe large portions of the working class as 'middle-class workers.' This change of terminology allowed me to better describe, categorize and analyze increasing proportions of the working class who, as professional, commercial, service and government employees, were 'middle-class workers' and indeed members of the working class. Their differences from laborers were in sociological categories such as educational attainment, cultural proclivities, leisure pursuits and their very places of work. However, they clearly shared with laborers the fact that they derived their living from wages and salaries. They had no control over money capital or fixed capital, nor managed labor power or owned the means of production. Nor did they participate in the creation and execution of state ideology and policy.

Social critics from Karl Marx and Friedrich Engels to E. P. Thompson and Erik Olin Wright have observed the multiple factions of the working classes (Thompson 1968; Wright 1997). Marx and Engels, in *The Communist Manifesto*, explicitly saw that capitalism had 'converted the physician, the lawyer, the priest, the poet, the man of science into paid wage laborers' (Marx and Engels, in Tucker 1978: 476). The Argentine workers I interviewed conform to the profile of the US worker today and, of course, this includes the new ranks of the for-profit digital workers. They live by the sale of their labor power and receive less than the value of the production and circulation of the goods and services in which they are involved. That is their commonality and their potential for indignation and rebellion.

The worker-ownership alternative

There is much reason to be positive about the feasibility, continuity and longevity of the major innovations among worker cooperatives and worker-recuperated enterprises. These constitute participatory worker involvement in managing enterprises, worker direct democracy through periodic assemblies, job rotations and reskilling and educational and cultural outreach to community groups, social movements and labor unions (Ranis 2005, 2006). The public policy oriented to neoclassical economic austerity has to be opposed by workers within their communities. The struggle has to be national in character and global in impact. The US working class must lead by example against the major capitalist purveyor of neoliberal economics and, if they are successful, other countries' working classes will take note.

Today's working class is made up of a majority of workers that are not unionized nor working full-time but rather: 1) are workers in danger of losing their jobs; 2) those who have already lost their jobs; 3) those who no longer are looking for a job; 4) those in precarious jobs; 5) those working in part-time, conditional jobs, including those in the digital economy; 6) youth about to enter a future without jobs. This is the combined dark outlook in the world of work. This is the context in which new forms of worker empowerment must be found.

In a world where corporate capitalism and forms of state socialism seem the only apparent alternatives, the various Occupy movements throughout the world, as well as the recuperated enterprise movements and cooperative developments in Argentina, Spain, Greece and elsewhere, have been joined of late in Cuba by a significant public initiative to form worker cooperatives. This push toward cooperative formations demonstrates forcefully the demands among workers in all forms of political systems to aspire to greater democratic participation in their lives and enhanced worker self-management in their working lives.

As OWS amply demonstrated, when multiple frustrations boil over, people from all walks of life do not wait for the advent of some magical revolutionary moment to vent their grievances. At a time of confronting corporate capital by way of democratic alternatives, the Occupy movements have offered added motivation for the working class to begin to consider their own earned space. Workers have the same legitimacy in the specific context of their place of work as the Occupy movements have to occupy public spaces. Workers, by dint of putting in decades on the job, should have the right to claim their enterprise or factory if and when the owners claim bankruptcy or decide to downsize, outsource or abandon their community in search of higher profit margins elsewhere. This is clearly the breach which working-class cooperatives can enter today. The rights to the urban commons that David Harvey writes of should be extended explicitly to the workplace itself, because it has become socially constituted labor property based on years of developing its capital (Harvey 2012: 72–3; Wolff 2012).

The Occupy movement in the US that resisted home foreclosures, tried to renegotiate student debt and rein in Wall Street financial prerogatives needed to also embrace the occupation of factories and enterprises that threaten to downsize, go offshore or declare fraudulent bankruptcies as they prepare to move to cheaper labor venues.

In Argentina over three hundred worker cooperatives formed with the assistance of municipal and provincial expropriations and other legal court interventions from recuperated enterprises now employ over 13,000 workers (Ruggeri and Vieta 2015). In the US we have the case of the New Era Cooperative that has grown out of Chicago's Republic Windows and Doors factory occupation and has begun production as an industrial cooperative. In Cuba, the government of Raúl Castro has had to embrace the cooperative worker alternative in the public dialogue by way of the new April 2011 Economic and Social Policy Guidelines for the Party and the Revolution formulated at the Sixth Communist Party Congress. There are already several hundred small worker cooperatives in the US and a number of state-dominated agricultural cooperatives in Cuba, and a growing number of cooperatives in services and commerce. But now there is an evolving understanding among public intellectuals, students and workers themselves that greater worker management and control of the workplace will lead to increasing democratization and efficiency that promotes national development under both capitalist and socialist models.

Cooperatives, whether in Argentina, Spain, Italy, Brazil, Uruguay, Venezuela, Cuba, Canada, Great Britain or the US, have the basic commitment to fulfilling seven characteristics that provide their working-class owner-workers with a minimum of justice and equity.

1. They are all-encompassing ideologically, absorbing different sectors and individuals of the working class, be they radical, progressive, liberal or conservative in outlook. They come together because they can agree on the need to confront unemployment and the economic deterioration of their communities. This provides

them with new motivations that not only alter their intellectual perspectives but also their ideological outlooks.

2. They constitute participatory worker involvement in managing enterprises, direct democracy through periodic assemblies, job rotations and reskilling of the worker. They eliminate targeted layoffs and end distinction between full-time and part-time workers. Profits and wages move together. In fact, in some preliminary way, wages become decommodified in cooperatives, in that they are distributed as shared rewards for collective efforts rather than on the basis of collective bargaining demands through labor unions or individual negotiations with an employer. Cooperative economic upturns and downturns are shared equally.

3. Within cooperatives, workers learn by the process of doing and learn quickly that their actions have consequences and ramifications. Information is no longer held by capitalist owners and managers as a wedge of power against workers but generously shared with any workers with a minimum vocation and appetite for enhanced understanding of the production process. Technological innovations are used to reduce onerous work and shorten the work week rather than as an excuse to lay off workers.

4. They share the potentiality of creating working-class autonomy and a sense of class consciousness based on the learned experiences in the process of production. Workers begin to conceive of themselves not as private individuals struggling to survive but as collectivities. Workers understand they are not merely consumers or ephemeral voters but members of a class. It is class consciousness born through everyday struggle in the workplace rather than an ideology that enters externally.

5. Cooperatives are clearly more likely to eliminate a two-tier wage structure while overturning existing de facto discrimination against women, minorities and immigrants. Since they focus on education and continual dialogue they are able to confront the biases inherent within typical capitalist firms. Bigotry, discrimination and gender biases become clearly counterproductive in an environment that focuses on survival through collective engagement.

6. They very often create working-class community solidarities beyond the factory or enterprise which serve to promote educational and outreach programs and the pursuit of collective leisure and learning environments, promoting the creative arts and

information of all sorts critical to a concerned citizenry. Worker cooperatives develop both interest and involvement in politics in association with their community's cultural, arts, healthcare and continuing educational activities. Community outreach is the default position of cooperative workers.

7. Once established, cooperative workers are available for wider struggles against repressive capitalist and state socialist policies. They are far more likely than trade unionists to support fraternal strikes, other worker occupations and working-class struggles outside their own workplace. They are less likely to see their workplace in isolation apart from other cooperatives and the society at large. It becomes the DNA reality principle of guaranteeing continuance. Worker cooperatives, as opposed to private hierarchical or state enterprises, are not likely to be reversible once organized because the members develop a keen sense of worker autonomy and decision-making as a real and long-term process. Worker cooperatives, once organized, are unlikely to leave their community because they develop a keen sense of local anchoring and defending their worker autonomy as a substantial working-place alternative. (Ranis 2014)

Though most cooperatives are collectives with decision-making undertaken by majority vote or by consensus, the larger cooperatives, necessarily, have a board of directors, selected by the whole membership, hold regularly scheduled and accountable assemblies and regularly scheduled elections. The key ingredient is of course that each member has the same single vote in all major decisions on wages, investments and economic outlook. In addition, in a huge cooperative corporation like the Spanish Mondragón as well as in the smallest cooperative, the wage differentials are held to a minimum and rarely exceed 4:1 based on contribution, knowledge and skills. On the other hand, as we have said, in the US Employee Stock Ownership Plans (ESOPs) owners hold the stock in the company on behalf of the employees, essentially for retirement purposes, and operating decisions are not under the control of the workers. They accumulate shares but have no say in how they are invested nor in the direction of the firm. In the final analysis ESOPs are not required to be run as democratic structures.

Thirty years ago, David Ellerman argued on behalf of cooperatives as examples of democracy in the workplace in their legal defense of the personal rights of worker-owners as opposed to owners' property rights of capitalist firms and employee stockholder shares within ESOPs. These personal rights of workers supersede viewing workers as commodities or marketable rights of property ownership. As Ellerman writes, 'worker-members are not employees because they do not sell their labor; they sell the fruits of their labor … it is their legal embodiment … In this manner, a proper legal structure will transform a company from a piece of property into a social institution wherein people will receive the fruits of their labor and have democratic control over their working lives' (Ellerman 1984: 267, 273). Years later, Ellerman argued strongly that the worker has an inalienable right not to rent himself out to an employer as if he were his property. The worker should have the right to choose the organization and institutional structure under which he/she will live. It can be delegated but the individual remains the principal (Ellerman 2015: 14). He goes on to write that the employee, whether individually negotiated or by collective contract, accepts a lesser legal rule. In essence the worker becomes a tool rented over a certain time period. Whether it's 'consent to alienation' or 'consent to delegation' it is not democratic (ibid.: 17).

A year after Ellerman's 1984 work, Robert Dahl wrote that democratically run economic enterprises are justified as much as justifying a democratic nation and are more achievable and more meaningful in the lives of men and women who spend at least 50 percent of their waking hours at work (Dahl 1985: 135). He added, '… in theory and practice both corporate capitalism and bureaucratic socialism have rejected the … principle of equality for economic enterprises' (ibid.: 117). He goes on to write hopefully, 'I cannot say whether a people … possesses the firmness of purpose and the clarity of vision to assert the priority of democracy, political equality, and the political rights necessary to self-government over established property rights, economic inequality, and undemocratic authority within corporate enterprises' (ibid.: 163).

In essence cooperatives represent democracy as a form of people's power rather than simply a capitalist state form of representative democracy or a state socialist form of democratic centralism. We have had the examples of the '*indignados*' of Spain, the Wisconsin worker uprising, the Arab Spring and the US Occupy movements – all testimony to the potential of workers' response to injustice and support of rebellion for democratic, participatory causes.

4 | ARGENTINA'S COOPERATIVE CHALLENGES AND BREAKTHROUGHS

[handwritten: How born the contemporary argentine industrial coop social and economic crisis]

Introduction

Contemporary Argentine industrial and service worker cooperatives were essentially born in the run-up to and during the massive popular societal demonstrations of December 2001. They owe much of their momentum to the social and economic crisis that offered little alternative to laborers and employees but unemployment and poverty. Factory and other enterprise bankruptcies and employer abandonment of places of work forced the laborers and employees to seek redress for their grievances. One of the measures to which they turned, inspired by two prominent worker organizations, was the formation of worker cooperatives, which are sanctioned by historical Argentine law. Forming cooperatives became only the first step in often long legal, community and political struggles that gave the workers temporary rights to re-enter the factories and enterprises and initiate or continue production and services. What follows is an appraisal of the capacity of Argentine worker cooperatives to maintain alternative norms of producing under capitalist economic constraints while providing an ongoing critique of traditional capitalist modes of workplace organization. In this respect, Argentina provides one of the most important examples of cooperative development within global capitalism and a major influential model of worker empowerment.

The Argentine worker cooperatives are not movements that have been able to mount a collective insurgency that would inspire one to recall the Paris Commune of 1871. Then workers for ten weeks sought to turn factories into democratically run enterprises throughout Paris in the latter days of the French defeat at the hands of the Prussian armies and the creation of the Third Republic. In those heady days of revolutionary struggle, the Paris Commune was elaborating a plan to turn all of Paris's factories and workshops that had been closed by their employers into an amalgamation of one large cooperative network. Of course, these decisions were made in the context of a revolutionary culture, temporary as it was, that sought to change the organs of indirect, parliamentary democracy for direct worker-led municipal councils, universal suffrage, the right of recall of elected representatives and a whole host of deep structural changes that were, within seventy-two days, aborted by the administrative, political and military powers of the national government at Versailles (Marx 1998 [1871]). What is also of interest is the variety of perspectives exhibited by the communards from anarchism to republicanism. They came together from a variety of backgrounds that fused into a movement that confronted the capitalist values of the day. What seemed to bind them all together was a sense of national patriotic unity and the desire to promote a workers' cooperative network throughout the length and breadth of France (Abidor 2015). These perspectives and orientations do bring us closer to the achievements and continuing goals of the Argentine cooperative and recuperated enterprise movements of today. As was the case with the brief experience of the French workers in the Paris Commune, Argentine recuperating enterprise workers were able to achieve a taste of the mystery of administrating an enterprise and of attaining firm viability without single leaders but rather through collective, shared responsibility.

Nor could one forget the societal upheaval during the dramatic months of 1936/37, during the Spanish Civil War. Then, in the regions of Catalonia and Aragón, under the auspices of the anarchist CNT, 2,000 industries were collectivized and taken over by rank-and-file workers. Municipalities abolished the currency and payment based on work hours was instituted, abortion was provided on demand, prostitution abolished and the women re-educated and 'revolutionary weddings' – simple unions between couples – became unremarkable. The struggle to win the war against a well-armed Fascist uprising collided often with the deeper aims of anarchists and Trotskyists for a socialist workers' revolution (Durgan 2011). The resulting fratricidal warfare, finally dominated by a liberal government, left the Spanish Republic bereft of a united front. Again, by 1939, the terrible revenge, repression and terror meted out by the military authoritarian regime of Francisco Franco destroyed this attempt at a deep cultural and societal revolution (Orwell 1952). The onset of Fascism in Italy under Mussolini, state socialism implanted under Stalin and military authoritarianism unleashed against the socialist government of Salvador Allende in Chile in 1973 are further testaments to the terrible challenges facing worker autonomous movements (see Wallis 2011).

Though Argentina experienced the heady days of 2002 when the watch words were '*Que se vayan todos*' (get rid of them all'), referring to the economic and political powers that be, the resultant caretaker policies of acting president Eduardo Duhalde and the return of a Peronist to office in (2003) restored Argentine 'normalcy' (Ranis 2004). The opening for a revolutionary change was, in retrospect, short lived and the return to liberal politics dampened hopes for a spontaneous proliferation of worker cooperatives.

Argentine society after the crisis of 2001/02, and particularly after the elections (2003, 2007 and 2011) of presidents Néstor Kirchner and Cristina Fernández de Kirchner from a newly formed Peronist coalition, Frente por la Victoria, has returned to the fold as a liberal democracy. Thus the possibilities of forms of working-class power, autonomy or special access have been marginalized. Civil society has always been a contested and troublesome terrain. Workers, though an overwhelming societal majority, have throughout history been unable to achieve political change that offered them advantages befitting their numbers and their contribution to the health and welfare of that same society. This has been amply perceived since the dawn of industrial capitalism. For example, for Hegel, civil society was a combination of the forces of individual desires dominated by economic interests. These needed to be refashioned and mediated by the moral code of the state. As he wrote, '[civil society] ... ...is in thorough-going dependence on caprice and external accident, and is held in check by the power of universality. In these contrasts and their complexity, civil society affords a spectacle of extravagance and want as well as of the physical and ethical degeneration common to them both' (Hegel 1942: 123). Marx, coming out of this Hegelian vision of civil society, was among the earliest analysts to fully encapsulate the material nature of civil society as divorced from the principles of political society and the claims of citizenship. In *On the Jewish Question*, Marx depicted the duality of the civil society where bourgeois self-interested motivations predominate and where people behave largely as individuals pursuing their personal and family interests. On the other hand, political society represents the mythic individual in whom community in citizenship triumphs over material concerns. In the spirit of Thomas Hobbes, Marx saw civil society as predominantly a 'war of all against all.' The public persona was transmuted into the private aggrandizing individual (Marx 1978). In this struggle it has always gone badly for the working class.

The post-rebellion Argentine context

Marx's notion of 'species being in community with other men' falls by the wayside as economic man inevitably triumphs. And high on that list of self-interest is the defense of private property so critical to John Locke's view of civil society. This became for the Argentine workers their most serious obstacle in recovering the factories and enterprises to which they had devoted many years of their lives. Once an enterprise is in default, the Argentine bankruptcy laws favor the primacy of creditors and the rapid auctioning of the factory or enterprise, its machinery, furnishings and supplies. It is at this point in the commercial litigation that the worker organizations and their lawyers, representing the locked-out workers, commence proceedings that allow for the worker cooperatives to temporarily occupy the factories in lieu of compensation for lost wages and benefits. Since at the time of the auction, as secondary creditors after the primacy of banking creditors, they would often be assured but 5 percent of what was owed them. It is a strategy that seeks to protect the basic property, machinery, patents, and copyrights from the auctioneer's gavel.

The Argentine community of civil rights groups, the residue of the once prominent neighborhood assemblies (which originated with the crisis of 2001), the immediate neighbors surrounding the factory or enterprise, assorted groups of unemployed workers who often picket to be heard (*piqueteros*), university and secondary school students, human rights groups and several small leftist political parties have all at one time or another pitched in to lend their support to the workers to prevent their ouster from their jobs and livelihood. The essence of community-based citizenship, which Marx described, becomes the means by which portions of society necessarily come to the aid of workers exercising their essential task of earning a living (Marx 1978). This is made absolutely necessary in Argentine society, where the balance of interests is tilted so strongly in favor of powerful economic interests with their predominant control over both capital and the state. Thus, in Argentine civil society, the prerequisites for and commitment to a just legal and economic order are still so distant that incredible efforts must be marshaled to attain minimal rights for the vast bulk of the working class. Marx correctly envisioned that existing civil society would be dominated by production and commerce and that these entities would be the chief concern of the state (ibid.).

Despite these historical and contemporary obstacles, the Argentine worker-occupied factories and enterprises represent a novel on-the-ground departure among social movements. They have the authenticity to flourish, embedded as they are in the survival responses of workers and the moral authority of maintaining national production through working-class employment. The 1990s, under the Carlos Menem presidency, had dramatically accentuated the devastating deindustrialization in Argentina that began during the military regime of 1976–1983. Within the first several years of his government, the country sold at bargain-basement prices the national enterprises of petroleum, gas, electricity, railways, hydroelectric dams, banks, the subway system, maritime and airline fleets, the most-traveled commuter highways, and radio and television stations (Ranis 2004). Under the aegis of overvalued dollar–peso parity, foreign investment increased significantly, as did foreign imports of all kinds of industrial products. While we witnessed a spiral of Argentine deindustrialization, investments abounded in utilities, services and the extractive economy. The demise of industrialization had a nefarious impact on domestic enterprises with a concomitant increase in unemployment, poverty and inequality symptomatic of a dual society (Rameri and Raffo 2005; Lozano 2005). The partial financial default of Argentina in late 2001 sharpened these conditions. The collapse of the peso convertibility severely affected smaller firms with higher levels of indebtedness, those that produced for the domestic market but often depended upon imported raw materials and supplies for their production (Kulfas 2003).

Even the positive growth rates since 2003, averaging just under 8 percent through 2013 (Página12.com.ar, 19 November 2014), have impacted only marginally on 80 percent of the Argentine population. Unemployment has improved, however, to 7.5 percent of the population, though 33.6 percent of the economically active people survive in the informal, non-unionized sectors of the economy, particularly in the areas of domestic work, the self-employed sector, and the salaried construction and commercial workers (Página12. com.ar, 12 December 2014), and those underemployed are at 7.8

percent (Pagina12.com.ar, 20 February 2014). In the state sector 42 percent of employees are considered precarious in that they are most often on short-term contracts of between six months and one year (LaNacion.com, 10 May 2015). In a country once dense with powerful unions, those in the salaried sector have a unionized density of 24 percent (Palomino 2010).

Whereas before the advent of the military dictatorship in 1976 the top 10 percent of social strata earned eight times more than the bottom 10 percent, that figure had increased to 17.7 times that of the bottom 10 percent (Pagina12.com.ar, 26 March 2015). Though poverty and indigence have fallen substantially in Argentina since 2002 (ECLAC 2012: 217–18; Pagina12.com.ar, 27 January 2015) income distribution continues to be among the most unequal in the world with a Gini index of .381 (Página12.com.ar, 26 March 2015). What makes an unjust society is much more about how unequal its class structure is than how many poor people it has. The former is a question of purposeful public policy, the latter a question of history, geography and resources. As Marx wrote so poignantly, '… the bowl from which workmen eat is filled with the whole produce of national labor, and that what prevents them fetching more out of it is neither the narrowness of the bowl nor the scantiness of its contents, but only the smallness of their spoons' (Marx 1975b: 7–8). In this respect Argentina remains among the more unequal countries in Latin America.

During the Argentine recession of 1998–2002, the societal indicators hit rock bottom. Poverty and unemployment soared to unparalleled historical proportions, with three-fifths of the population poor or indigent and a third without full-time employment. The crisis accentuated pre-existing patterns and behavior among the owners of small and medium-sized Argentine industrial firms and commercial establishments. The worker-occupied factories and enterprises did not proliferate in a vacuum. They are a direct result of the Carlos Menem governmental policies that allowed workers to be fired and laid off, with limited severance packages, if management could prove to the Ministry of Labor that the firm's viability was endangered. In essence, Argentina's labor flexibilization laws allowed the owners of these firms to reconfigure the workplace to enhance productivity and to restructure their workforce based on market rationales (Ranis 1999). These policies, combined with the recession that began in 1998 and the default crisis of 2001, created a miasma in the world of work and the Argentine working class (Itzigsohn and Rebón 2015). Many of these firms started proceedings that would end in default to their creditors and outright declarations of bankruptcy. Invariably, in the cases in which workers chose to occupy their factories and enterprises, there was overriding evidence that the industrial recession was often fraudulently used by the owners to decapitalize their firms. They obtained millions of dollars in government credits, often used for non-production-related financial speculation, and, ultimately, deprived the workers of their earned wages as they broke the labor contracts and simply walked away from the factory or enterprise (Kulfas 2003: 8–19). As these neoliberal policies deepened in the 1990s, a portion of the Argentine workers seized on the methodology of taking control of factories and enterprises that were being decapitalized by their owners and/or were in various stages of debtor insolvency or outright bankruptcy. Worker-occupied factory and enterprise cooperatives became a clear alternative to unemployment and poverty (Di Marco and Palomino et al. 2003; Fajn 2003; Cafardo and Domínguez Font 2003; Rebón 2004; Ruggeri et al. 2005; Vieta 2009; Ranis 2006, 2010; Itzigsohn and Rebón 2015).

Argentine worker-recuperated enterprises confront the neoliberal system

In the wake of these abhorrent conditions, two Argentine worker organizations were founded which attempted to organize and motivate workers to take over their factories and enterprises and then use moral suasion, political pressure and legal strategies to maintain control over their means of production and provision of services. The Movimiento Nacional de Empresas Recuperadas (MNER) was founded in 2002, and the Movimiento de Fábricas Recuperadas por los Trabajadores (MNFRT) was founded in 2003. Their goals were similar: to create a belt of worker cooperatives throughout the country. Their strategies differed and will be amplified below. In recent years, estimates of the number of enterprise occupations vary from as few as about 200 with 8,000 laborers and employees to as many as over 311 with approximately 14,000 workers (Ruggeri and Vieta 2015). The wide fluctuations are because some estimates cover factories and enterprises that have been researched and documented and others that have as yet not been documented but are reportedly managed by the workers. More importantly, as the takeover process is often surrounded by bankruptcy filings, prolonged litigation and occasional municipal and provincial legislative expropriation measures, the definition of a worker-occupied enterprise is dependent upon the author's understanding as to whether the enterprise is fully a stable worker-run enterprise or one still in the process of formation.

The Argentine bankruptcy law permitted, as one alternative, the formation of cooperatives with national, provincial or municipal government involvement. In May 2002, in the midst of the economic crisis, an important additional reform of the bankruptcy law allowed for the bankruptcy court trustee to rule that workers could initiate production in the enterprise, if a majority of workers so agreed. The law permitted the factory or enterprise to continue to be an integral whole until such time as the factory could be auctioned off to a new buyer. Obviously, this constituted a very unstable situation among the workers willing to continue production via a workers' cooperative, since they were not guaranteed any priority at the time the factory was auctioned off. At this point, the workers, in consultation with legal advisors and the two umbrella worker organizations dedicated to recuperating enterprises, began asserting the provisions of the national and provincial constitutions of Argentina that provide for the right to work in any lawful industry, the right to strike for lost compensation, and which allow for the expropriation, duly compensated, of private properties on behalf of workers for reasons of the 'common good' and 'public use' (Briner and Cusmano 2003: 26–30). In a major victory for thirteen occupied factories located in the capital city of Buenos Aires, the municipal council passed legislation in November 2004 that made permanent the rights of the worker cooperatives to maintain control over their enterprises. The legislation stipulated that the machinery, the trademarks and the patents should belong to the workers. The workers were given three years of grace to begin paying over twenty years, in six-month installments, the value of the firm at the time of the bankruptcy, not the enhanced value added by the workers at the time of the expropriation. Prior to this blanket permanent expropriation authorized by the municipality, there had been individual company expropriations on a provisional, two-year basis in several Argentine provinces, predominantly in the province of Buenos Aires via its provincial legislature. In the absence of legislative intervention, other cooperatives have restarted production under judicially arranged rental agreements. This is particularly prevalent in cases where the previous owner has abandoned his property.

In June 2011, a new bankruptcy law (26.684) was passed by the Argentine National Congress, introducing seemingly positive reforms of the previous bankruptcy law (24.552) that built on a previous law harkening back to one promulgated under the military dictatorship in 1983, its last year in power. The new law gives priority to workers, when two-thirds of the workers agree to organize as a cooperative to carry on the enterprise or factory in lieu of lost wages and severance packages, allowing the bankruptcy judge to allow the cooperative workers to purchase their company. As Luis Caro argues, the revised law determines the protection of sources of workers' employment and the continuity of production as central rights and defends the rights of workers to receive compensation for past losses of wages and benefits, whereas before the 2011 bankruptcy law, workers' right to work was always secondary to the rights of property (interview, Luis Caro 8 May 2014). However, the new law still gives much arbitrary discretion to commercial court judges in awarding the company to the cooperative workers and forces workers to continue to return to their most propitious historical avenue, namely to pursue temporary or permanent expropriation of the firm by Argentine provincial or municipal legislatures (Ruggeri and Vieta 2015).

Legally sanctioned expropriation avoids the fear of the owner and creditors coming back to make claims on the enterprise. Workers forming cooperatives make the claim that they are owed severance pay, often months of missed pay checks, lack of social coverage, including pension, 'aguinaldos' (year-end bonuses) and healthcare (obras sociales). Expropriation provides protection from creditor demands on the previous owner's debts. Without expropriation, creditors can demand the auctioning of the building and its contents to pay the owed debts. Once provincial or municipal legislative expropriation is in place creditors must go through the courts to recover their debts. The municipality or province takes charge of dealing with the creditors. In most cases these public authorities have not provided the monies to fully compensate the creditors. Until there is a national expropriation law in Argentina, many cooperatives will continue to seek continuance of grace periods at the municipal and provincial levels.

The great majority of worker-managed enterprises are in the metallurgical (including appliance and auto parts), food processing, meatpacking and allied industries, textiles, printing, graphics, ceramic and construction industries, and restaurants, as well as, though in smaller numbers, in hospitals, health clinics, private schools, hotels, supermarkets, pharmacies and other services. Fifty percent of the factories and enterprises are in the capital and Greater Buenos Aires, which have traditionally been the industrial center of Argentina, and another 15 percent in the province of Buenos Aires, comprising 60 percent of all the cooperative workers. But what is very important is the spread of recuperated enterprises to the remainder of Argentina, now comprising 35 percent of recuperated enterprises and 40 percent of the workers. The growth of these cooperatives has continued unabated in the recent 2010–13 period (Ruggeri and Vieta 2015). In a recent survey of 156 recuperated factories and enterprises throughout Argentina, a team of investigators found that 95 percent of the recuperated workplaces were cooperatives and that three-quarters of them had fifty workers or less. The overwhelming majority produce for local domestic consumption at levels averaging 50 percent of potential capacity, though some plants do better than others, mainly in the metallurgical and food processing sectors. Significantly, the average wage level in the worker cooperatives was US$250 a month, which is substantially above average Argentine salaries and five times unemployed welfare payments to the *piqueteros*. What is particularly noteworthy is that two-thirds of the recuperated enterprises have histories that date back to the halcyon days of Argentine industrial growth between 1940 and 1970 (Ruggeri et al. 2005). This era of import-substitution industrial national development was abrogated by the military regime of 1976–83 and continued under the weakened state system of the Raúl Alfonsín presidency. A clearly neoliberal economy was then initiated by the administration of Carlos Menem and promoted under the structural adjustment reforms of the Washington Consensus.

In approximately the same time period as the Ruggeri study, Julián Rebón wrote up his investigation of recuperated enterprises limited to the capital of Buenos Aires. Its data provides a nuanced assessment of the processes and outcomes of the cooperative phenomena as understood and implemented by its worker participants. The underlying message of the study was that the workers, whatever their ideological predispositions and levels of class consciousness, were essentially resisting unemployment to the best of their capacities. It comprised an intensive investigation of seventeen of the twenty-six recuperated enterprises within the city of Buenos Aires. Sixty-two percent of them were involved in industrial production, with the balance mainly in the service areas, including hotels, restaurants, schools, and health clinics. The majority of the workers were skilled laborers as opposed to technical or unskilled workers (Rebón 2004). Nationwide, Rebón has estimated that among recuperated enterprises there is a mortality rate of about 15 percent, but that is more than compensated by the formation of new cooperatives each year (interview, 16 July 2007).

The MNER has been led by Eduardo Murúa and José Abelli and the MNFRT by Luis Caro. Between the two associations, the former was more national and was heavily represented in the capital city of Buenos Aires; the latter more ensconced in Greater Buenos Aires, which includes the surrounding industrial suburbs in the province of Buenos Aires. In interviews with the three leaders in July 2004, with Murúa in July 2006 and with Caro in July 2005 and July 2006, it became clear that they have much in common in their critiques of the neoliberal economy and the irresponsibility of both the corporations and the Argentine government. They recognized the conundrum of a surplus-labor economy and an increasingly competitive international environment that foregrounds major downsizing and asserts race-to-bottom pressure, particularly on small and medium-sized capitalist enterprises. The MNER, under the leadership of Murúa, ex-member of the left-Peronist Movimiento Peronista Montonero, made the connections between the US Treasury, the World Bank and the IMF as the source of the austere, corporate-driven Argentine national economic policy. On the other hand, the MNFRT under Caro avoids politicizing the issues and takes a more task-oriented, case-by-case approach that applies various legal and self-help measures to initiate the enterprise recuperating process. Symbolic of the differences between the two workers' organizations are their representative slogans. The MNER created the image of strength through outreach and solidarity by way of 'to occupy, to resist, to produce,' borrowed from the Brazilian landless peasant movement Movimento dos Trabalhadores Sem Terra. On the other hand, the MNFRT promotes a more pragmatic approach that focuses on self-sufficiency and autonomy by way of 'to work, to produce, to compete.' Since 2005, Argentina has seen a proliferation of other recuperated-enterprise worker associations, formed from splits from the MNER and MNFRT. José Abelli, in association with Fabío Resino of the Bauen Hotel cooperative, formed FACTA (Federación Argentina de Cooperativas de Trabajadores Autogestionados), metal worker union locals led by Barba Guttiérez formed MERBA (Movimiento de Empresas Recuperadas de la Provincia de Buenos Aires) and, under the auspices of the CTA labor confederation, ANTA (Asociación de Trabajadores Autogestionados) was formed.

As José Abelli told me, 'We have destroyed all the rules of economics. We only had human capital. In some recuperated factories we began with only US$100. In many cases we have tripled to quintupled the number of workers. Salaries have multiplied by ten times in some cases. We have created a virtuous circle' (interview, 21 July 2004). On the other hand Murúa has argued for clear national expropriation legislation that could encompass the 10,000 enterprises that have gone bankrupt and allow the workers a chance at reviving them. Murúa argued that this, along with a moderate subsidy per worker involved in cooperatives from the Ministry of Economy or Labor, would regenerate thousands of jobs. He argued: 'Workers can produce without capitalists; but capital cannot be produced without workers. Cooperation can supersede competition at being productive' (interview, 8 July 2006). On the other hand, Caro, of the MNFRT, expects little governmental support in the way of subsidies and chooses the road of labor sacrifice within the cooperatives during the first few months of takeover while saving the salaries of former managers, who often earned between ten and twenty times the wages of the average worker.

For Caro, it is of crucial importance to maintain the Argentine factories and enterprises in operation. If the factory is abandoned or sold as property without the workers, the experiences of its employees and the tools lost, the whole country is the poorer. 'An axle-wheel is sold as scrap iron, but for a worker this axle-wheel provides work for three people: the lathe operator, the assistant and the apprentice. The judge can sell it all; but I believe in a new deal, a new contract, without disregarding the creditors or the owners, one that gives the workers the opportunity to use their resources to pay off the property' (interview, 19 July 2005). At the same time, Caro is a proponent of using the various provisions of the provincial and federal constitutions, which, he argued, would trump the national bankruptcy law, which was, at the time of the interview, far less favorable to the workers' interests (interview, 24 July 2006).

Meanwhile Caro had advocated for a reform of the Argentine national bankruptcy law (*Ley de Quiebras*) of 1995, which had put workers at a severe disadvantage. He had argued successfully at legislative hearings about the inequity of workers' claims being secondary to the debts owed to the banks and suppliers by the closed enterprise. A factory bankruptcy traditionally favored the previous owners, the creditors, and the court-appointed trustees, who sought to move toward bankruptcy in order to attain their healthy commissions of up to 12 percent. Once it was auctioned, purchasers could buy equipment at bargain-basement prices to resell later at huge profits. And, of course, should the factory or enterprise be reconstituted, none of the workers was guaranteed a job. For all these reasons, expropriation would be a far better outcome for the workers because it avoids the possibility of the owner (and sometimes the creditors) coming back. This has allowed the workers to begin to share in the cooperative's profits in lieu of the lost severance pay and social coverage (pensions, *'obras sociales'* and *'aguinaldos'*). As Caro argued, bankruptcy gave the workers at best only 50 percent of what was owed them in indemnization, often as little as 5 percent once the assets of the equipment and machinery had been sold off. Under the previous bankruptcy law, Caro argued, 'The workers' twenty to thirty years of work is sold for a pittance at a rigged auction … The workers have a constitutional right to strike, remain in the plant because it is my factory, my home, my livelihood, defending my work and my machinery; what I have built up and I remain to protect this from the owner emptying a place of potential production' (interview, 24 July 2006).

Expropriation gives the cooperative workers protection from the creditors' demands upon the previous owner who incurred the debts. Without expropriation creditors can demand the auctioning off of the building and its contents, while throwing the workers into the streets. Creditors must now go through the provincial courts to make their claims. It is for these reasons that Caro and his colleagues argued for case-by-case expropriations, which are most likely to curry the favor of commercial court judges. He doubted that a national law of expropriation was on the horizon. He argued that 'With expropriation there has to be compensation' (interview, 24 July 2006). At the worksite, once the cooperative is formed, Caro argues that workers banding together can usually make a go of it. Often up to 80 percent of the cost of paying the profits and salaries of the owners and managers is eliminated. Moreover, cooperatives are spared paying sizeable taxes on enterprise profits. Additionally workers can decide collectively to reduce their wages in the first months of recovery while utilities and most suppliers need not be paid until the end of each month.

Overcoming political and economic challenges to the formation of worker cooperatives

Argentina is recognizably a liberal democratic capitalist political economy and recuperated enterprises and cooperatives at large recognize this reality. There is no way to minimize the challenges and struggles that Argentine cooperative workers have faced and will face as they pave a new road to worker autonomy and self-respect. On the other hand, cooperative formations offer a genuine progressive alternative that begins to undermine root-and-branch capitalist entitlement. As this chapter has shown, each of the many obstacles to workers' ownership and management of their workplaces can be met and overcome by workers' own imagination and willpower.

Overall, until the two Kirchner governments, the dominant political and economic institutions of contemporary Argentina were not supportive of a major worker cooperative movement. Though it maintains a sympathetic hold on public opinion, which favorably contrasts the hard-working cooperative laborer or employee with the *piqueteros* on welfare, the national administration was not overly sympathetic and only nominally supportive via very minimal per-worker subsidy from a sub-secretary's office of the Ministry of Labor, which in most cases involved having to go through a series of technical and bureaucratic hoops before a worker even qualified for the nominal subsidy. In addition, limited subsidies have occasionally been forthcoming on an ad hoc basis, largely from the Ministry of Social Development (Ministerio de Desarrollo Social) and the Municipality of Buenos Aires (Ruggeri et al. 2005; interview with Eduardo Murúa, 26 July 2004). According to Cecelia Casablanca, representing the Ministry of Production, since 2004 the municipality of Buenos Aires has given limited subsidies and assistance in such areas as equipment purchase, hygiene, commercialization, infrastructure, and technical training, because it argued that the cooperatives lack expertise (interview, 24 July 2006). Within the Ministry of Labor, the Secretary of Employment's *Programa de Trabajo Autogestionado* has two minimal subsidy programs for workers involved in enterprise cooperatives: 1) to help them in the early stages of forming a cooperative, during which they provide grants of US$50 per worker; and 2) once the cooperative is legally recognized and has come up with a complex document and ministry-approved production plan, another US$170 is provided for each cooperative worker. These subsidies provide little substantive support (interviews with Silvia Mercedes Rebón and Cristina Teijeiro at the Secretary of Employment, Ministry of Labor,1 and 15 July 2005).

Since early 2006, the municipality of Buenos Aires has created a Sub-Ministry for the Social Economy directed at supporting projects in the informal economy that lead to the creation of mini-enterprises, such as in textile and food processing. The formation of cooperatives is one of the major goals. Once it was organized, the city of Buenos Aires established contracts to purchase supplies such as hospital sheets, public school uniforms and school lunches. The sub-ministry provided small subsidies of US$1,000–2,500 to newly formed cooperatives (interview with Hugo Fucek, executive director, 26 July 2006). These subsidies and subsidized technical assistance plans point up a major shortcoming for Argentine cooperatives. In contemporary Argentina, there are few predictable lines of bank credit available to the cooperatives, so they must depend on the unpredictable and arbitrary decisions of public officialdom to give them one or another ad hoc and one-time subsidy. Fucek, later as head of the Unión Productiva de Empresas Recuperadas, has argued that connections between cooperatives and governmental ministries need to be expanded. He pointed out, for example, that the printer cooperatives could easily supply 70 percent of books needed by the Ministry of Education for distribution to the public schools (Fucek 2011). Virtually no bank, public or private, ventures to give cooperatives or recuperated enterprises loans because in many cases they lack the financial accounting history, modern technology and explicit market plans – all generic questions that don't always fit their profile (interview with Ramiro Martinez, spokesperson for a recycling waste cooperative, Recuperando el Trabajo (Recovering Work), 27 July 2006). And once more, with public subsidies, the cooperatives have to provide accounting for every peso spent, whereas with a commercial line of credit the cooperatives would establish a degree of autonomy on how they implement the money.

Until the presidency of Cristina Fernández de Kirchner (2007–15), the offices of the presidency, the Ministry of Economics and the Banco de la Nación gave only occasional pro forma audiences to representatives of cooperative worker organizations, but in reality they placed them low on their radar screen. Equally daunting was the deleterious neglect on the part of the national legislative and judicial powers. Edith Oviedo, president of a children's book publisher cooperative – Cefomar – plaintively saw the national government as 'deaf, dumb and blind' to the needs and potential of Argentine cooperatives (interview, 25 July 2006). In the vacuum of national legislation, it is particularly the adjudicating court judges and the court-appointed trustees who, during the conflictual stages of a company's insolvent debtor proceedings and subsequent bankruptcy filings, present the greatest obstacles to the workers taking over the enterprise, committed as they are to the fundamental priority of the sanctity of private property. At the same time the business community is clearly suspicious of the worker cooperatives. On the other hand, in cases of conflict between the cooperatives and their former owners, the surrounding factory or enterprise community, the *piqueteros* and sectors of the legal, political and human rights associations come to their aid in terms of moral, political and technical support.

Absent from these worker support groups, with few exceptions such as the printers' union and some metallurgical, ceramic and pharmaceutical union locals, is the Confederación General de Trabajo (CGT), the massive Argentine labor federation. It has been uninvolved and has essentially kept its distance from the plight of the workers' cooperatives in sustaining their factories and enterprises (interview with Javier López, executive secretary of ANTA, the cooperative federation within the Central de los Trabajadores Argentinos (CTA), the alternative labor confederation, 27 July 2007). The CGT apparently sees the move to recuperate employment as an epiphenomenon of neoliberal economic adjustments for which they won't sacrifice their relationships with the employer class. Their structural vision is that of representing fully employed, dues-paying members, not those who have left their web of representation. The CGT seems caught in a time warp in which unions negotiate with employers for minimal pay increases in return for ever-increasing benefit give-backs while minimizing massive downsizing of the formal labor force. Ignored entirely in this posture are the majoritarian informal workers that now include the cooperative laborers and employees. Since the cooperative workers are, in essence, their own bosses, the trade union movement can't seem to adjust to that structural characteristic. At the same time, the CTA has also, until recently, remained aloof, focusing on questions of economic income redistribution rather than a revision of the relations between capital and labor (ibid.). Owning their own means of production puts the cooperative workers in a kind of representational limbo. This requires the cooperative worker organizations to focus their attention on changes in public policy as opposed to a reorientation of the union outlook.

The challenge to the worker-occupied enterprises is that, usually upon the takeover, many administrative personnel have left with the owners and managers. This phenomena, though it saves huge administrative costs, often requires major adjustments and a learning curve for the workers in the first months of the takeovers. Many cooperatives, because of their conflictual histories, often have to pay suppliers in cash, have difficulty establishing new credit lines, and many work with raw materials provided by the contractor (à façon). Another area that naturally confronts the newly managed worker enterprises is the severe lack of investment capital and access to the market. However, once these challenges are met, the worker solidarity and sense of competence are usually greatly enhanced. In my interview with the leader of an umbrella worker organization, it is clear that the first months of the enterprise recuperation require great sacrifice and commitment in terms of labor hours, deferred pay, reaching out to previous suppliers and establishing continuing commercial contacts with retailers (interviews with Luis Caro, 13 July 2005 and 24 July 2006). And, since often the newly established worker cooperatives depend upon large capital enterprise suppliers, this can act as a major roadblock to reinitiating production. On the commercialization side they do better, since two-thirds of their customers are small and medium-sized establishments, social entities, other cooperatives and sympathetic consumers at large. Under these conditions, most recuperated factories and enterprises I visited would like to have community outreach programs but circumstances make this difficult. In many sites, the workers are too exhausted from their labors, their obsolete machinery needs replacing and often they are undercapitalized without the necessary labor force to undertake these societal outreach programs. Pablo Heller makes the further argument that many cooperatives are so underfunded that they are forced to auto-exploit their workforce under onerous conditions (interview, 26 July 2005, and Heller 2004).

Decades ago, Antonio Gramsci wrote that political society and civil society reinforce each other to give advantage to certain strata, groups and institutions. Civil society remains more hegemonic than free and is based on a manufactured consent (Gramsci 1971: 206ff; Buttigeig 2005: 6). Though the leaders of the Argentine cooperative workers' movement and their professional and legal support base serve in some sense as Gramsci's 'organic intellectuals,' the worker cooperatives continue to survive and develop in an uneven playing environment. Conditions make it difficult for the workers to assert freedom and independence from the dominance of public policy-makers. The cooperatives are certainly not beyond the governmental, administrative and juridical reach of the state. In fact civil society is the arena in which the ruling stratum extends and reinforces its powers and legitimacy (Buttigeig 2005: 26). The cooperative movement in Argentina is fraught with serious challenges that sometimes seem overwhelming, but that the workers continue to confront them with a combination of boldness and ingenuity. Nevertheless, as will be assessed in subsequent chapters, the Argentine cooperative movement continues to make gains, and recruit new workers who understand that cooperatives provide a positive alternative to the clear and present danger of unemployment and poverty.

5 | ARGENTINA'S LEADING EDGE

The Zanón ceramic tile and porcelain factory of Neuquén Province is perhaps the bellwether of the movement to recuperate abandoned factories in Argentina. Though it has formed itself into a cooperative called FaSinPat (short for Fábricas sin Patrón – Factories without Bosses), it still advocates for an eventual national ownership with worker control instead of the cooperative enterprise approach. The Zanón workers argue that expropriation without compensation is the essentialist goal since payment would reward fraudulent behavior by the owners at the expense of the economic wherewithal directed at the community and the society at large. From the 1990s the Zanón family contracted debts of approximately $120 million with the World Bank and several Argentine banks before declaring insolvency in 2002.

According to Mariano Pedrero, past legal advisor to the Ceramic Workers' Union of Neuquén (El Sindicato de Obreros y Empleados Ceramistas de Neuquén), they advocated for an independent social movement that put the Zanón factory at the service of the community and not the market. As opposed to what he called 'the islands of worker cooperatives' trying to survive, the Zanón workers wanted to use the recuperated factories as a wedge to develop a social movement on behalf of societal change. Pedrero saw the Zanón experience as an example of John Holloway's 'changing the world without taking power' (interview, 13 July 2006). In the eyes of the Zanón workers change requires expropriation – 'nationalization under worker control.' Pedrero argued that 'If there were a hundred Zanóns this would be a different country. Zanón is struggling not to be just another factory but to be the leading edge of social change in Argentina' (interview, 7 July 2005).

The Zanón ceramics factory has managed not only to preserve the workplace but to add to national productivity and to create employment, while reaching out to its surrounding community (Magnani 2003: 132–58). Its internal egalitarian organization and community outreach make it a standard of worker self-management and community relations. Since 2002, when the factory takeover took place, the factory has gone from 260 to 475 workers and has greatly increased its production. It has excellent relations with the local university, the *piquetero* organizations and the civil society at large by way of its community center, health clinic, employment of those in need and its multiple cultural, artistic and recreational outreach programs, which often include 10,000 people, many of them directed at the children of the city of Neuquén. In addition, the Zanón workers continually make donations of free tiles for building projects for schools, hospitals, childcare centers and individual families in great need, including Mapuche Native Americans living in Neuquén (Workers of Zanón communiqué, 19 September 2008; Aiziczon 2015).

Though political conditions under Presidents Néstor and Cristina Fernández de Kirchner and Governors Jorge Sobisch and Jorge Sapag made expropriation of the plant without payment and under worker control an unlikely prospect, the workers continued to defend that vision (interviews with Mariano Pedrero, 7 July 2005 and 13 July 2006). Nevertheless, the workers' militancy combined with solid community support finally achieved the expropriation of Zanón as a cooperative by the Neuquén provincial legislature on 12 August 2009 after nine years of working-class struggle. The province of Neuquén took on the commitment to compensate the creditors. Finally, in January 2014, the Zanón cooperative was given formal title to the factory, which greatly eased its access to credits and allowed the necessary renovation of its machinery.

Distinct from the many Argentine labor unions that have not supported worker cooperatives, the Zanón Ceramic Workers local branch won majority control in 1998 against the former bureaucratic union that was in collusion with the owner. One of the union leaders, Raúl Godoy, recounted that the former union leadership all had a price for their collaboration with the former Zanón owners. A shop steward delegate's price was $30,000 dollars, the president of the local branch $60,000 dollars. 'The more activist you were, the workers thought, the higher the price for his collaboration.' In this climate of co-optation and fear, the oppositional union group began conversing via lunchtime soccer games with future delegates who were transmission belts of information, support and solidarity. Once the previous union leaders were defeated in union elections in 2000, they called on the provincial legislature to auction off the

Zanón factory so they could get the indemnization owed them. The new Ceramic Union leaders led by Godoy were continuously 'red baited', creating a perilous adversarial relationship within the Neuquén provincial legislature. As recounted to me by Godoy, after winning union control, the Zanón management, accustomed to buying off the former union leadership, offered them the union dues collected over three months as a bribe. 'We gave them two minutes to leave or we would kick their ass' (interview, 14 July 2006). This, in itself, made the Zanón cooperative cohesive as the union took a leadership role in strategic and tactical decisions. Once it represented the workers, the union was instrumental in confronting an ever more repressive owner administration, leading to the factory occupation of 2002. The makeup of the union leadership was also extremely important since it consisted of several highly influential members of a Marxist political party, the Socialist Workers' Party – Partido de los Trabajadores Socialistas (PTS) – which advocated for nationalization with worker control.

According to Pedrero, of the 475 workers in Zanón at the time, approximately fifteen are PTS members while another 150 ceramic workers are consistent activists in planning the factory mobilizations and outreach. The remainder of the workers are supportive. They continue to promote the thesis that worker autonomy is not negotiable and that workers can direct social, political and economic policy for the good of the greater society. There is little doubt that the interaction between the PTS cadre and the rank-and-file Zanón workers was a crucial element in their enduring struggle against what seemed insurmountable odds centered in the opposition of both the Argentine provincial and national governments as well as the threatened capital formations in Neuquén and within Argentina itself. It is only the ability of these workers to organize the city and surrounding communities of Neuquén that has allowed this ceramic factory to survive and prosper. In my visits to Neuquén and the Zanón factory in 2005 and 2006, I saw clearly the ostensible commitment of this left leadership to a moral and incorruptible stance on both internal factory questions and its relationship to the outer community. They consistently applied direct democratic procedures in the running of both the union and the factory. The factory assemblies were and are assiduously held and the union shop stewards debate the issues democratically with high levels of rank-and-file participation. When they had openings at Zanón the union gave priority to the various organizations of the unemployed *piqueteros* as well as family members of the ex-ceramics workers fired by the former owner (Aiziczon 2007: 17). It is very significant that in 2006 an 'independent' union leader, Alejandro López, won the union election replacing Raúl Godoy as general secretary, though they evidently share their anti-bureaucratic, democratic and participatory orientation.

The Zanón cooperative has been able to engage the Neuquén community. In protests initiated by public sector employees, public school teachers, nurses or the students of the National University of Comahue (Universidad Nacional de Comahue), the Zanón workers always offer their workforce for the demonstrations. Their message, which includes a clear cultural outreach along with their political message, is a distinct part of their overall strategy. Significantly, the Zanón workers extended a major commitment to the largest unemployed workers' organization – the Movimiento de Trabajadores Desocupados (MTD) – which exemplified their societal consciousness and outreach (Aiziczon 2015: 8).

Each week they present three fifteen-minute radio programs to counteract the provincial press and radio stations favorable to the Neuquén Popular Movement (Movimiento Popular Neuquino), a very conservative, majoritarian party that dominates the provincial polity. Godoy, as sub-secretary general of the Zanón Ceramic Union leadership, explained: 'Zanón moves on two legs – production and politics – they go together or they don't go at all' (interview, 14 July 2006). While Alejandro López, the Ceramic Union general secretary, said: 'When we have to support another struggle, we stop production because it is a social investment, a sowing that we reap in the future' (interview, 15 July 2006). They see productivity as means to a larger goal, as part of the working-class struggle for greater power and recognition within society. Moreover, they stand out in that they send sizeable supportive delegations to national cooperative mobilizations and meet with counterparts at conferences from western Europe to Venezuela. Since the global recession of 2008 and beyond, Godoy has visited western Europe and met with workers and cooperative workers in France, Greece and Spain, depicting the struggles and successes of the Zanón workers.

Since the failed attempt to shut down the factory and lock out the workers in 2001, the Zanón workers have successfully managed an impressive democratically run factory. All policies are made by majoritarian decisions of weekly run assemblies. In addition, once a month production is halted for an eight-hour discussion among the workers concerning procedures and goals. No leadership position is permanent, and the constant rotation of positions of responsibility is a hallmark of this cooperative. Workers in production, sales, or administration earn the same monthly salary. However, those responsible for such key areas as maintenance of the machinery and those who safeguard the factory at night and on weekends receive an additional 10 percent over the basic salary. In addition, each month, if they meet their production goals, all workers receive a production bonus of approximately US$80 added to their base pay of US$600 a month. The organization of the workday is very distinct from that of the prior Zanón family management. At that time workers in each sector had to wear different uniforms that prevented them moving out of their designated areas, couldn't talk or listen to music while working, nor could they drink maté on the job. All this has been reversed (interview with Alejandro López, general secretary of the Zanón Ceramic Union, 15 July 2006, and Godoy's presentation to Greek workers at the Viome cooperative factory in Thessaloniki, Greece, 24 May 2013).

Leaders and delegates can be revoked by a simple majority vote and terms of office have been reduced from four to three years. The workers' assembly remains the highest organ. In the cultural arena, Zanón does not dismiss workers for ideological or religious reasons, only malfeasance, proven neglect of the machinery and products or a consistently unexplained absenteeism. Before the Zanón workers' occupation and takeover, there were approximately three hundred annual work-related accidents, whereas under worker management this had been reduced to thirty-three accidents and none of the serious variety (Aiziczon 2015: 15).

Women make up 10 percent of the workers. They receive paid maternity leave – forty-five days prior to the birth and forty-five days after the birth. In addition, mothers are allowed to begin work one hour later and go home one hour earlier. We learned from Vanessa Jaramillo, spokesperson for the Zanón factory women's section, that the Zanón women are also major activists among the *piquetero* organizations, peasant groups, state workers, teachers and university student movements (interview, 15 July 2006). According to Jaramillo,

Abortion is still illegal in Argentina. But women ignore it. There is still no free distribution of contraceptives or sexual education. Machismo attitudes remain. Many of the women in the factory are still opposed to abortion. It's a debate that people are still very hesitant to talk about. Both the Catholic and Evangelical churches maintain lots of influence, even if Neuquén is relatively progressive because of the existence of many social movements. For example, many *piqueteros* are women (70 percent) so that we ally with them in the various struggles to find employment – this brings them out of their very individual characteristics into a more collective behavior. (Ibid.)

The Zanón workers see their factory as being at the service of the community and not the market, and that attitude has been translated into countless acts of solidarity, for which they have been compensated by the community in five attempts by the provincial police to take over the factory. Zanón workers are battling not just to be a workers' cooperative factory but, also, an incipient movement inspiring social change (Ranis 2006). They argue that an effective state must take responsibility for creating jobs while allowing workers to control production and extend its surplus to the whole community. Historically, when the Zanón workers have initiated a protest to call for provincial expropriation without compensation, they have always organized a mass movement that mobilizes vast sectors of the communities of the city of Neuquén, which inevitably influences the political culture of that city. I witnessed their demonstrations in July 2006 and can attest to the support the workers received from the provincial Universidad de Comahue students, public school students, teachers, nurses, and public sector employees.

The impact of the Argentine cooperative development can be seen by how its recuperated enterprise movement has been referenced by factory occupation workers in Greece, Spain and Italy. For example, Raúl Godoy spoke to Greek workers occupying the Viome factory in Thessaloniki, Greece, reiterating the important lessons in the workers' decade-long struggle to own and manage an abandoned factory with debts left by the former owner of Zanón. He stated in clear terms that 'the workers' assembly decisions are the heart of the struggle,' since it is an investment in time that is crucial not only for decision-making but for future mobilizations and worker commitment and solidarity. Godoy spoke eloquently of the day-long assembly held once a month that halts work to discuss the factory's financial accounts, its budget income and outlays and future investment and capitalization policies. The workers of Zanón had learned how important the years of struggle had been for the workers' learning curve in confronting capital and the state. He recognized that as successful as the Zanón workers' cooperative has become, individual cooperatives cannot be guaranteed long-term survival without the continuous struggle to establish a socialist society based on worker cooperatives (interview, 24 May 2013).

Godoy and Alejandro López also demonstrated their ideological commitment to solidarity. As part of a left-party coalition known as the Frente de la Izquierda y de los Trabajadores – FIT (Left and Workers' Front), they won a seat in the Neuquén provincial legislature. They will rotate the seat each year for the four-year term, keeping the same salary they would have earned as ceramic workers, the balance added to a strike fund for other workers' labor conflicts and those in need in the community of Neuquén. Their argument is that the legislative process is one additional arena in which to improve public education, housing, healthcare and struggles against unemployment.

On 12 August 2014, the Donnelly offset printing factory of 400 workers in the province of Buenos Aires followed in the footsteps of Zanón by occupying their factory a day after the US multinational printer locked out the workers and declared fraudulent bankruptcy, although data was available showing that they were a leading profitable company in the Argentine graphics/printing sector (Bayer 2015). The commercial court judge allowed the bankruptcy on a single weekend without an exploratory investigation, and President Fernández de Kirchner even called it '*quiebra express*' or fast-track bankruptcy (Meyer 2015). Most of the non-administrative personnel, comprising 230 workers, entered the factory and began claims for back pay, indemnization and the company's previous cutoff of their health coverage. They received the rights to form a cooperative under INAES registration and called themselves Cooperativa Madygraf, named after the daughter of one of the workers who had made a recovery from a severe illness, just as the factory would recover from its present crisis (interview, Eduardo Ayalla, Madygraf (ex-Donnelly) cooperative president, 30 October 2015). Once established, the cooperative received the support of university faculty and students in training some of the workforce to undertake new administrative responsibilities (ibid.).

After twenty-two years in the province of Buenos Aires, Donnelly, with 55,000 workers and 600 plants worldwide, with half in the US, abruptly and inexplicably terminated their investments in Argentina. The projected cost-cutting wage policy had been opposed by the factory shop committee and a week before the closure the workers strongly opposed the laying off of 123 workers. This obviously led to the bankruptcy decision by the owners.

Donnelly printed many popular magazines such as *Gente, Para Ti* and publications of Editorial Atlántida, as well as documents issued by the Argentine national ministries of labor, education and health. As in the Zanón example, Madygraf workers were able to receive the support of the progressive sectors of Argentine society, such as various university student bodies, the surrounding communities in the province of Buenos Aires, left-party members of the national and provincial Chambers of Deputies and public opinion at large. In a conscious effort to demonstrate their social awareness and impact, the cooperative printed and distributed gratis 10,000 notebooks for schoolchildren in the surrounding towns in the province of Buenos Aires (interview, Jorge Medina, dissident delegate of the former printers' union, 30 October 2015). The cover depicts the workers protesting at the entrance to the factory after the lockout. The cooperative has become a cause célèbre and they have managed to start production once more and received a temporary expropriation through the lower house of the Buenos Aires provincial legislature on 20 May 2015, but this has not been followed by the provincial senate and it appears to be on permanent hold, given the victory of a conservative, neoliberal governor of the province of Buenos Aires and president of Argentina, Mauricio Macri. Like Zanón's, the Madygraf position favored 'nationalization under worker control' but adopted a worker cooperative approach as the best possible outcome given the limits of state intervention and ownership within a liberal capitalist system.

The Hotel Bauen stands as perhaps the most serious iconic commercial cooperative challenge to Argentine private business-as-usual because of its location on the corner of two of the major thoroughfares of Buenos Aires, the avenues of Corrientes and Callao. The twenty-story hotel was built at the height of the military governmental repression in 1978 in anticipation of the World Soccer Championship held in Buenos Aires. The former owner, Marcelo Iurcovich, incurred multiple loans from governmental and private banks during the military regime, and later the Menem government, and used these credits, as the Argentine economy began to falter in the late 1990s, to invest in other hotels and financial markets. The owner, after successive firings of the employees, sold the hotel to a Chilean firm, which paid only a third of the $12 million owed Iurcovich, and by December 2001, in the depth of the economic crisis, he claimed bankruptcy, throwing the remaining workforce of eighty into the streets. At that time, the son of the original owner, Hugo Iurcovich, asked the commercial courts to reinstate the family ownership (interview, Diego Ruarte, founding member of the Bauen Cooperative, 30 October 2015). However, he never reimbursed the banks for the original loan agreements and thus was not awarded the hotel. In essence, the hotel still belongs to the Argentine government's Banco de la Nación, which has never been repaid their original loans. The strategy of the private owners of the Bauen Hotel was to avoid paying their state debt by selling the hotel to partners and family members and thus be clear of their debts and start afresh, often with new workers (interview, Federico Tonarelli, vice-president of the Bauen Cooperative, 2 November 2015). At the same time the Bauen workers, via an injunction, filed for and received a temporary two-year expropriation so that the worker cooperative could reopen the hotel.

In March 2003, under the organizational prodding of Eduardo Murúa of the MNER, seventeen of the former hotel employees entered the hotel and began to restore its bar and lounge and eventually rehabilitate its rooms (interview, Eva Lossada, president of the Bauen Cooperative, 31 October 2015; she had just been re-elected on the very day of the interview by a vote of 68–42). Lossada had begun work at the Bauen Hotel as a chambermaid in 1994! By 2006 the Bauen Cooperative had restored 80 percent of the 160 rooms for tourism and had 150 workers, many, as is the cooperative tradition, family members of the hotel employees. The post-2008 global financial crisis impacted the Bauen, and as of 2015 the hotel employed 117 workers (ibid.). In the early stages of the recuperation, many employees lived in the hotel so as to save on meals and commuting expenses. Among the earliest guests of the hotel were cultural groups from Venezuela, funded by the national oil company PDVSA, which provided early stimulus for the hotel renovation. The hotel was skillfully commercialized, rehabilitating the cafeteria, bar and bookstore and slowly the available rooms. During my several visits to the hotel, culminating in my staying at the Bauen in 2015, it always seemed to be a meeting place for students and professionals as well as a hub for cultural, musical and intellectual activities. Very early in the restoration they received progressive tourism from both within and outside Argentina that allowed the cooperative to continue their work and begin the process of rehiring their labor force. During the rehabilitation, the employees worked for very basic wages so as to allow the cooperative to reinvest the profits in restoring more and more of its cafeteria and commercial and residential space (Fields 2008; interview, Diego Ruarte 31 October 2015). As with many of the recuperated enterprises, the Bauen workers, via the weekly meetings of the elected cooperative council, had to decide between increasing employee salary dispersals and reinvesting the basic surplus capital into the assets of the hotel (interview, Eva Lossada, 31 October 2015). At the time of my stay at the Hotel Bauen in 2015, the passenger elevators ceased functioning for several days and the workers had a major crisis on their hands that required an investment of approximately one million pesos to acquire a new system, while they made daily repairs.

The Bauen cooperative experience continued in legal limbo, particularly since the municipal elections of 2007 resulted in the election of the neoliberal mayor Mauricio Macri and a conservative majority in the Buenos Aires municipal council (interview with Fábio Resino, delegate for Bauen, 28 July 2007). In March 2014, the Bauen was again confronted with a commercial court judge's decision that the hotel had to be vacated by the cooperative workers and available to the previous owners, who had purchased the hotel with loans, never repaid, provided by a defunct bank under the military dictatorship in 1978. Federico Tonarelli, vice-president of the Bauen Cooperative and president of FACTA (Federación Argentina de Cooperativas de Trabajadores Autogestionados), argued that a national expropriation law was long overdue to allow the state to take over the factory, allowing the workers to rent the hotel facilities and keep the hotel productive. There were various proposals in the National Congress, although none had the necessary support to produce a national expropriation law (*Página 12*, 28 March 2014). However, in November 2015, in the last days of the Cristina Fernández de Kirchner government, an expropriation law finally passed the Chamber of Deputies, though it has not passed the Argentine Senate and, should it pass, it will most likely be vetoed by the newly elected neoliberal president, Mauricio Macri, former mayor of Buenos Aires (Vales 2015).

In its decade-long struggle for expropriation and recognition as a cooperative, the Bauen Cooperative never received the support of the gastronomic union of Argentina, a notorious union with a corrupt leadership. The Bauen Cooperative felt that this union, like most of the CGT unions, tended to negotiate primarily with the employers and then present the collective bargaining proposals to the rank and file rather than reaching an agreement among the workers before presenting collective bargaining demands to the employers.

In its organization the Bauen Cooperative paid the same minimum wages to all (approximately one thousand pesos a month, but additional supplements were granted for thirteen coordinators (administration, reception, dining room and bar, maintenance, room services, security, etc.) as well as for punctuality, employee transportation costs and subsidies for children). In contrast to Zanón, the Bauen began with practically nothing. The former owners 'took out everything and what they couldn't take away, they destroyed.' The courts provisionally allowed them three of the hotel floors because of community pressure, 'assuming we would fail and that we were just ignorant types who were going to spend their time drinking maté' (interview, Eva Lossada, 31 October 2015).

What has essentially kept the worker-managed hotel in operation, as with the Zanón cooperative, is the community support, solidarity from other cooperatives, and political support from leftist political parties and sectors of the human rights and legal communities. The multiple dimensions of the Bauen workers' success in keeping the hotel in operation for thirteen years have become the basis of continuing political and community struggles that encompass multiple allies in Argentine civil society and have demonstrated the power of the workers' collective mobilization and political acuity. Throughout the years of their struggle the Bauen workers were able to publicize the government's unwillingness to permanently expropriate the hotel with payment because it relied on temporary provincial expropriations without payment. For Tonarelli, this was a step too far for a democratic capitalist state (interview, Federico Tonarelli, 2 November 2015). Thus juridically, the Bauen Cooperative is still in legal limbo, but its support base encompasses social movements, other cooperatives and the progressive community, which provide it with legitimacy. As Tonarelli said, 'the Bauen is for all. The old Bauen Hotel was private. The new Bauen Cooperative is open to the whole society and every political social faction knows this and uses its "public" spaces.' In reality, he argued, it is not private property because it still belongs to the state, since it was never reimbursed by the original private capitalists (ibid.).

The Chilavert printers' cooperative represents another emblematic experience in the Argentine cooperative movement. As in the history of so many cooperatives, the previous owner took out large loans which were invested in personal ventures and then declared insolvency. It is then the enterprise that has to answer to the bankruptcy. Prior to the bankruptcy declaration there is a '*convocadores de creditores*' in which there are attempts to resolve the financial crisis, during which the workers are legally permitted to organize as a cooperative. During this period, the owner tried to empty the printing establishment of its most valuable printing presses. And in the declaration to the creditors, the owner had already erased these two presses from the inventory. According to Ernesto González, president of the Chilavert Cooperative, this represented collusion between the trustee of the commercial court and the owner of the enterprise – a common experience in Argentina (interview, 25 July 2005). The interim solution is dependent on the quite arbitrary decision of the judge to allow the workers to maintain the enterprise with a rental agreement with the former creditors. Again, only expropriation allows for a long-term solution for the workers, during which they are able to get back to work and begin to accumulate some assets.

Chilavert's leadership and small contingent of over a dozen employees recognized the pressures to take on the values of the larger society and act like any other small business trying to thrive. Most of their profit comes from the publication of magazines, advertising pamphlets and catalogues, but their steadiest income is from the printing of social science, literature and art books. In order to develop their foothold in the market they formed an inter-cooperative federation – Red Gráfica Cooperativa – with other printer cooperatives such as Gráfica Patricios, Campichuelo and Gráfica El Sol, to work with a collective, complementary and supportive approach, in a real sense embarking on a mini social economy. In their further societal outreach Chilavert has undertaken distinct programs that set them apart from the more limited outreach programs of many other cooperatives. They have created a Center of Documentation for Recuperated Enterprises and baccalaureate programs for youth and adults. In addition, Chilavert runs multiple cultural and historical programs for their community, some especially directed at primary and secondary school students in the areas of graphic and industrial arts (interviews with Cándido González and Martín Cossarino, members of the Chilavert shop committee, 4 August 2004 and 10 July 2006). Their extra-economic focus is largely on enhancing societal understanding of the cooperative movement in Argentina as well as engaging public policy.

Besides the recuperated enterprises and cooperatives presented in this chapter, I visited six metallurgical factories, a food processing factory, a food snacks factory, a meat-packing plant, a clothing factory, a furniture factory, a shoe factory, a shipyard building plant, a hospital, a children's publishing house and a primary school in Greater Buenos Aires, between 2004 and 2007[1] (see Ranis 2010).

Recuperated enterprises as well as cooperatives have become an often expected outcome in contemporary Argentina. During the crisis post-2001, and now under more normal economic conditions, recuperated enterprises have been the default solution when a private firm declares bankruptcy, the employer abandons the firm or in other ways removes machinery and produce, pays late or not at all, or stops contributing to health coverage and other labor benefits. The national government has apparently decided that expropriating the companies would be too expensive so they have increasingly allowed bankruptcy court judges to accept the formation of worker cooperatives to

1 For example, I visited Cooperativa Forja San Martín, Cooperativa de Trabajo San Justo, Cooperativa Los Constituyentes, Industria Metalúrgica y Plástica Argentina (IMPA), Cooperativa MVH/ex-Metalúrgica Vicente Hermanos, Polimec, Cooperativa Vieytes/ex-Ghelco, Cooperativa de Trabajo Malvinas/ ex-Don Matias, Cooperativa Yaguané, Cooperativa 18 de Diciembre/ex-Brukman, Cooperativa de Trabajo Maderera Córdoba, Cooperativa de Calzado Puporé, Astilleria Naval Unidos, Hospital Israelita, Cefomar and Instituto Comunicaciones.

allow production to continue and maintain employment. As one cooperative administrator has called this phenomenon: 'forming a cooperative has become naturalized' (interview, Ramiro Martínez, 23 October 2015).

Under these changing conditions, the Argentine Ministry of Social Development and the Ministry of Labor have increasingly, under the Kirchner administrations, become more involved in supporting the viability of cooperative survival. For example, the Ministry of Social Development has made large purchases from cooperative suppliers of shoes and uniforms for governmental workers, and government-sponsored cooperatives are organizing increasingly prominent social programs in public works in parks, street maintenance and construction under the name of *Argentina Trabaja* (reminiscent of the US New Deal under President Roosevelt). However, within these cooperatives, known as *Obras Sociales de Base* – Public Works Cooperatives – created as top-down public policy measures, the workers are payed as state employees rather than sharing profits as is customary in recuperated enterprises and niche societal cooperatives. The Ministry of Labor has a program called *Programa de Trabajo Autogestionado* – Program of Self-Managed Work – which provides modest subsidies to cooperatives for commercialization incentives, purchase of essential raw materials, machinery renovation, worker training and security and hygiene measures.

Argentine worker cooperatives: a growing phenomenon

Recuperated worker-owned and operated industrial and service enterprises remain the most celebrated and acknowledged societal labor movement in Argentina in the post-crisis years, yet other cooperatives of all types of origin abound in Argentina in multiple urban and rural economic niches in far greater numbers, many formed as state-sponsored public works, housing and construction. In addition there are many agricultural, public utilities and consumer savings, credit and insurance cooperatives. Collectively they contributed 9 percent of Argentine national GNP (Página12. com.ar, 14 December 2009). Cooperatives have existed in Argentina since the 1920s, mostly in the agricultural, consumer, credit and public utilities areas. However, since the 1990s and the economic crisis of 2001, the creation of worker cooperatives has been preponderant, with estimates suggesting that as many as two-thirds were formed in those six years (interview with Ramiro Martínez, vice-president of Recuperando el Trabajo – Recuperating Work – 23 July 2007). It is estimated that in the year 2012 alone over 6,000 cooperatives were formed under the Cristina Fernández de Kirchner government's Ministry of Social Development in part-time work in water and sewage treatment, cleaning parks and streets and housing construction (*La Nación*, 10 March 2013). This surge in cooperative development, of course, is not one of recuperated enterprises, but represents top-down government-sanctioned employment policies different from the ethos of cooperatives built from below by activist unemployed workers.

Many Argentine worker cooperatives originated in 2002/03 in the depth of the economic crisis that beset Argentina with rampant unemployment and spreading poverty among the poor, working and middle classes. They are distinct from recuperated factories and enterprises since they were initiated by the collective interests and efforts of the participants and represent entirely new business ventures. Several of the worker cooperatives I visited in 2005, 2006 and 2007 came about through incredible sacrifice and commitment. One such clear example is the Cooperativa La Cacerola, a bakery and restaurant cooperative, founded in 2003. It originated from unemployed workers that made up 90 percent of the Asamblea Popular (Popular Assembly) in the Almagro district of Buenos Aires. These popular assemblies proliferated during the depths of the economic crisis with the slogan '*Que se vayan todos*' (Sitrin 2012). In the early days of the subsequent Duhalde government, followed by the Kirchner administrations, it became clear that the Peronist liberal democratic leadership had returned and that the people had to essentially rely on themselves and pull themselves up by their own bootstraps. The Almagro assembly chose to avoid the route of public assistance (*planes familiares*) and created a consumer cooperative for vegetables and fruits bought collectively from farmers' markets (*mercado acópio*) and distributed to its 100 members. They organized their own markets and traded goods and services among themselves as an interim barter club that lasted two years and existed on the edge of the money economy.

At this point one of the assembly members, a master baker, was about to lose his baking machinery. The neighborhood assembly occupied the tiny premises and eventually collectively reached a rental agreement with the commercial court judge. Along with the master baker and an unemployed former bank loan officer they formed the nucleus of a bakery. They began hiring, the only prerequisites being to be unemployed and willing to work hard, demonstrate solidarity and be pluralistic and tolerant of distinct points of view. With the help of Eduardo Murúa and the MNER, they found two small abandoned warehouses which the Buenos Aires municipality subsequently, as the owner, allowed them to use. In return, as a newly formed cooperative, they established a relationship with the city to provide certain needy public schools with lunches, eventually supplying 2,000 prepared meals. With a loan from the Banco de la Nación of $10,000 dollars, they began hiring new workers and expanded to establish a restaurant on the premises, and by 2007 had over thirty employees. No doubt the unusual success in achieving this loan came from the fact that the loan solicitation was made by the cooperative treasurer, Walter Blanco, himself a fired bank loan officer. Blanco (president of La Cacerola, 2010–12) described how they opened up a second floor dedicated to cultural events, buying the furniture and tiles at reduced prices from other existing cooperatives, including the Zanón ceramic cooperative. In 2004 they participated in the formation of Mesa – Movimiento de Economía Social Argentina (Argentine Social Economy Movement), coordinating fifty such small- and medium-sized cooperatives and other small enterprises, essentially in food and textile production, and have created a weekly *feria* (open market equivalent to farmers' urban markets) in which they sell to the general public (interview, Walter Blanco, 20 July 2006).

By 2015 the Cacerola Cooperative was continuing to grow with forty-four employees working in three shifts daily with a functioning cafeteria, bar and a very active cultural center with almost weekly events directed at the community and cooperative issues of the day. They have a contract with twenty-five Buenos Aires public schools to provide them with 3,400 box lunches. They also provide box lunches for events at the nearby University of Buenos Aires Faculty of Philosophy and Letters. They serve customers with over forty bakery and dessert items such as cookies, bread and rolls, pizza, cake and pies, empanadas and mixed grill sandwiches. It is a cooperative success story based on participatory worker involvement and rotation of responsibilities.

Fifty percent of their income derives from public school programs and Philosophy and Letters students at the nearby University of Buenos Aires. In addition, at the many cultural events held in their upstairs dining room, they sell food and drinks. In addition, under the Kirchner government's Ministry of Culture neighborhood events, they often served thousands of attendees (interview, Silvia Díaz, president of La Cacerola, 2003–10 and 2012–14, 31 October 2015).

Like Cooperativa La Cacerola, another example of what Argentines call *cooperativas de base* is Creando Conciencia – Raising Awareness. It is an ecologically concerned and environmentally sustainable recycling cooperative founded in 2007 just north of the city of Buenos Aires. These are cooperatives created to provide employment and fulfill a niche in the economy that provides needed services and income. This cooperative recycles garbage by collecting, separating and compressing glass, plastic bottles, and paper products from gated communities known as '*countries*' in Argentina, which prefer to work with private carting companies rather than the public collectors. After their collections and processing they sell the compacted refuse to porcelain factories, paper industries, plastic bottling plants and fruit juice container manufacturers. They now have plans to recycle plastic items into plastic lawn chairs for sale (interview, Ramiro Martínez, organizer and spokesman for Creando Conciencia, 23 October 2015).

In 2010 they had one truck for garbage collection and recycling; now they have five trucks. Between 2010 and 2015 the cooperative had expanded from employing fifteen workers to employing thirty-three. There are three elected leaders on the administrative council – president, secretary and treasurer – and an administrator who follows their guidelines. Once each year they hold an annual assembly to discuss production, investments and fiscal balances, etc. (*Memoria y Balance*), although the president, Edgardo Herman Jalil, makes clear that there is an ongoing dialogue and almost weekly meetings at breakfast, lunch and during breaks that are informal but instructive. The average wage is 8,000 pesos monthly, approximately $800 in 2015, while the floor for beginning wages is 6,000 pesos. The wage gap among the workers based on complexity of the job, responsibility and seniority rose from 3:1 to 4:1 by 2015 (intervew, Edgardo Hernan Jalil, 27 October 2015).

The workers' cooperatives have in most cases become self-help, autonomous struggles in which workers share equally in the profits and share equally when sustaining losses. Via worker assemblies the workers are well informed and they collectively make the major decisions on investments, work schedules and work rotations. Antisocial behavior is addressed and work malingerers and 'free riders' are fired, but only after documented repeated offenses. Worker alienation is significantly muted as they feel they are literally working for themselves and are their own bosses. When orders drop, instead of firing workers they all submit to a pay cut across the board until things improve. In that sense they are stakeholders as well as workers. They realize, having essentially been abandoned by most labor unions, that they are in a risky business and must depend on their own resourcefulness to survive. Though they have had important connections with other recuperated enterprises within the MNER and MNFRT, community organizations and the progressive left, with occasional municipal contracts, they still live in a challenging environment.

In conclusion

Since chronic, structural unemployment and poverty confront the workers on a daily basis, their cooperative construct is developed to a high level of intercommunication and consensus-building, since they are only as strong and viable as their weakest link. Their autonomy and independence from the former owner-employers, unions and state supervision sets them free from traditional monetary relationships. It is fair to say that in a microcosmic way the cooperative workers have replaced the liberal motto of 'a fair day's wage for a fair day's work' with the 'abolition of the wage system' (Marx 1975b [1865]: 78). As the worker cooperatives struggle to occupy, recuperate and maintain their factories and enterprises they must necessarily depend not only on community support but also upon people politically and legally knowledgeable about their rights and prerogatives.

The Argentine government, even under the progressive Kirchner administrations, still works under a benevolent national bourgeois notion of politics that provides a clear intent of stabilizing a capital–labor relationship – a kind of political Keynesianism. It is essentially a continuation of the traditional Peronist ideology of social justice – *justicia social* (Ranis 1995).

As it has been posited since Hegel and Marx, civil society is essentially bourgeois society. Argentine workers must actually claim that, in establishing cooperatives and in defending their places of work from the auctioneers, their demands are an essential part of that very bourgeois fabric of civil society. They need to become conversant with bankruptcy laws, and provincial and federal constitutional provisions. And they need to argue along lines that convince bankruptcy court judges and trustees that their capacity to run a factory or enterprise is sustainable and capable of turning a profit, as opposed to the practice of past creditors in simply selling off the installation and its contents by way of an auction. In order to reach these jurisdictional arenas, the workers have often resorted to 'semilegal' actions of factory and enterprise occupations and resistance to being removed. At that stage they depend upon lawyers and civic activists who support and defend their grievances. As Chatterjee writes in the context of India, 'these groups, organized into associations, transgress the strict lines of legality in struggling to live and work.' He accurately depicts such groups as living within 'political society' but outside of what is conventionally thought of as 'civil society,' replete with access, influence and legitimacy (Chatterjee 2004: 40ff.). Within political society, *piqueteros* are picketing and blocking highway and street commerce to make their demands while workers struggle to form cooperatives. Both are attempts to push civil society's governmental leaders to evolve and expand their understanding of the meaning of civil society and who deserves rights within it. As Chatterjee reminds us, 'Property is the crucial dimension along which capital overlaps with the modern state' (ibid.: 74–5). And in that often unequal struggle, workers and their community and legal advocates must seize on every democratic claim to justice, equity and reasonableness to achieve their significant goals.

6 | THE PROLIFERATION AND INTERNATIONALIZATION OF THE ARGENTINE COOPERATIVE EXPERIENCE

By 2015, Argentina contained a virtual gamut of almost 39,000 cooperatives, most of which were not worker cooperatives, but gas, water, electrical and telephone utility cooperatives, savings and credit union cooperatives and insurance and medical mutual cooperatives (Area Estudios y Estadística: Informe 4to. Trimestre, INDEC, 2015). Within this total number of cooperatives, the Ministry of Social Development, under the two Kirchner governments, with the cooperation of Argentine municipalities, formed 20,000 cooperatives as societal outreach programs to create and maintain employment. These workers were engaged in housing construction, parks beautification, repairing schools and hospitals and various personnel services such as guards, watchmen and as personnel caretakers. Another 19,000 traditional cooperatives were made up of mutuals, housing, agricultural, consumer, credit, insurance cooperatives and include, the subject of this book, the nearly 7,300 worker-owned and operated industrial and service cooperatives of which approximately 367 are worker-recuperated enterprises, employing 16,000 workers, that represent the contested history of struggle with their former employers, the courts and the state itself. This includes recuperated factories and enterprises that have achieved rental agreements with former owners in lieu of indemnization for back pay; also, under 'cram-down' provisions, former owners have agreed to give up the factory or enterprise in return for the worker cooperatives assuming the employers' debts. There are also approximately four hundred cooperatives, such as La Cacerola and Creando Conciencia (discussed in the last chapter), that are known as Autogestión Asociativa Autónoma (Associated Autonomous Self-Management). Among all these cooperative developments it is estimated that fewer than 5 percent fail! (interview, Franca Venturi, coordinator of the Programa de Trabajo Autogestionado in the Ministry of Labor, 3 November 2015). As we have indicated in the last chapter, there are also several thousand public works cooperatives sponsored by the Argentine government to enhance employment and avoid poverty for large sectors of the *piquetero* movement (see below). Much of the continual growth of cooperatives may also be because of the new bankruptcy law of 2011, which gives the workers an immediate and legitimate opportunity to vote in favor of forming a cooperative. According to Franca Venturi, it puts commercial court judges into public view in determining with objectivity the rights of the workers under a company's proclaimed bankruptcy (ibid.).

INAES – Instituto Nacional de Asociativismo y Economía Social (National Institute of Associations and the Social Economy) – the technical administrator of the whole range of cooperatives, under the auspices of the Argentine Ministry of Social Development, registers the cooperatives, provides small subsidies to purchase hardware and tools and provides technical assistance throughout the country. Under the *Argentina Trabaja* mantle, many thousands of state-sponsored public works cooperatives work in the public sector of infrastructure maintenance, reconditioning and beautification of parks and roads and construction. Once formed with the political support of the various municipalities, the cooperatives approach INAES to register (interview, José Orbaiceta, director of INAES, 2 November 2015). The Argentine state, on the other hand, in regard to recuperated enterprises and niche-based, autonomous cooperatives, sees its role not as an originator of cooperatives but as a facilitator once the workers initially develop the venture (ibid.).

INAES is a decentralized institution with a budget of almost one million pesos, 50 percent of which comes from the Argentine Ministry of Social Development and 50 percent from the dues of the affiliated cooperatives. Orbaiceta estimates that, counting all the cooperatives in Argentina, they represent 10 percent of the gross national product. They represent a significant portion of the huge numbers of the small and medium-size firms that make up the bulk of Argentine employment (ibid.). Thus it is clear that cooperatives of all kinds are very much embedded within Argentine civil society and that recuperating enterprises, despite their conflictual challenges to capital and the state, are a recognized minority element within the cooperative political economy.

Despite the increasing support of the Ministries of Social Development and Labor, there is still clear neglect from the key economic ministry. This resulted in a leader of one of the two worker organizations – the MNER – Eduardo Murúa, traveling to Venezuela in mid-April 2005, where he attended the Third International Solidarity Congress in Defense of the Bolivarian Revolution, sponsored by the Venezuelan National Workers' Union (UNT). As an invited guest speaker, Murúa spoke of the Argentine experiences of worker-occupied factories and enterprises to a very receptive audience of 500 trade unionists. One of the major themes of the conference was 'worker co-management' in Venezuelan enterprises, and one of the slogans was 'without co-management there is no revolution.' Co-management was indeed intended to characterize the Argentine initiatives in running their factories, namely co-participation in production decisions, improving working conditions, setting egalitarian wage policies and collectively organizing the enterprise and commercializing its products. During his stay in Venezuela, Murúa also had a favorable hearing from President Hugo Chávez, in which the Argentine pointed to the more propitious environment for worker-managed enterprises in Venezuela under a worker-friendly government. Chávez acknowledged that he was interested in the Argentine experience, since he was looking for a way to bring together small and medium-sized business owners with workers to recuperate abandoned Venezuelan enterprises, with the proviso that they establish asset- and profit-sharing mechanisms with the workers. Murúa significantly added that the workers must control the enterprise policies as well as supervise its accounts in order to assure that the firm has collective outputs and goals. Murúa also pointed to the special presidential initiatives available to President Chávez and his opportunity in Venezuela to put worker control on the agenda throughout Latin America. Because of Chávez's interest in the Argentine experiences in recuperating factories and enterprises, Murúa was able to leave his MNER-written bill of national expropriation that has not been given support in the Argentine Congress. Significantly, by May 2005, the UNT had elaborated a proposed law to be forwarded to the Venezuelan Congress that put worker co-participation in industrial enterprises on the agenda; and indeed, in July 2005, Chávez proposed government financing at low interest rates to 700 closed factories and to 1,149 factories partially paralyzed since the 2002 economic crisis, if they would grant co-management and profit-sharing to their workers. The Venezuelan government will promote these factories as cooperatives or 'social production enterprises.' As in Argentina, the Venezuelan national constitution allows for the expropriation with just compensation for reasons of 'public use or social interest' (La Nación.com.ar, 15 July 2005).

Very dramatically, the Venezuelan government and its Chávez-allied labor federation (UNT) subsidized and sponsored the *Primer Encuentro Latinoamericano de Empresas Recuperadas* (1st Latin American Meeting of Recuperated Enterprises) at the end of October 2005. No doubt the impetus came from the Argentine MNER, which sent the largest delegation to the three-day conference in Caracas. Significantly, Hugo Chávez opened the meetings before several thousand delegates, interested elected officials, unionists, the press and observers. His inspirational speech of two hours addressed the creation of a new network of recuperated factories and enterprises throughout Latin America, parallel to the Venezuelan-sponsored and funded Petro-Sur and Tele-Sur. He envisioned an *'Empresur,'* to which the government has committed a US$5 million budget. He took the opportunity during his presentation to announce the expropriation of three Venezuelan firms on behalf of its workers.

The meeting, which I attended as a guest observer, included 700 workers representing over 250 enterprises from eight Latin American countries spearheaded by delegations from Argentina, Venezuela, Brazil and Uruguay. The focus of the meeting was the contemporary challenges of existing public policy, production obstacles and community outreach. During the three days the delegates met in cohorts of workers whose firms were prepared to exchange raw materials and products, explore new markets, exchange technological and scientific information and extend fraternal, financial and cultural cooperation. Additionally, there were meetings of both labor union and governmental and legislative representatives to explore means of assisting the evolution of recuperated worker enterprises. In three short days, seventy-five commercial agreements were signed among various Latin American worker enterprises in such areas as tourism, wood and paper production, food production and processing, shoes and footwear, plastics and transport.

Within Venezuela, this level of commitment to cooperative formation was exemplified by the existence of a Ministry of the People's Economy (MINEP), now the Ministry of Communal Economy (MINEC). Given the lack of such initiatives and funding from the Argentine government, this was a major breakthrough for the legitimization of this belt of worker-managed enterprises in Argentina, as well as in Venezuela, Brazil and Uruguay, where parallel worker cooperatives, mixed enterprises and state-owned and worker-controlled factories and enterprises have recently developed. The proliferation of cooperative formation, particularly in Venezuela, but also in Brazil and Uruguay, has continued since 2006. In Venezuela the investment in cooperatives is the most massive in Latin America. For example, the various state-owned banks invested one billion dollars in cooperatives between 2003 and 2008. With the state coffers open, 274,000 cooperatives registered in 2009 but only a quarter of them were officially certified as cooperatives, half in the service sectors of the economy. Perhaps more than in any Latin American country, cooperatives proliferated as enterprises to receive largess; others were paper cooperatives for the sole purpose of reducing their tax burden. Dario Azzellini writes that many Venezuelan cooperatives continue as capitalist enterprises, fully adopting the capitalist logic of maximizing profits and ignoring societal solidarity. In an effort to localize cooperatives and develop their responsibilities, the Venezuelan government in 2008 created the Social Production Enterprises (EPS) in which the Communal Councils work with cooperatives based on community needs. The Chávez government continued to tweak the cooperatives to better enhance their responsiveness and effectiveness, and realized that community and local relationships produce the best results (Azzellini 2013: 267ff.).

The Argentine government's lack of clear resolve in funding and supporting worker-managed factories and enterprises may exemplify an economic outlook that determines that public policy acts on behalf only of such entities with recognized and significant market power. Some micro-lending with long-term low interest rates and generous grace periods exists from long-standing and more recently inaugurated internationally based financial organizations, which focus on lending to cooperatives and small enterprises attempting to find niches in domestic markets in Third World countries, inclusive of Argentina. For example, there is The Working World in the US, Oiko Credit International of the Netherlands, Consorzio Etimos of Italy and ECLOF of Switzerland (interview with Ramiro Martínez, 23 July 2007). Though these international lenders to small cooperatives and enterprises have substantial resources and committed aspirations to eliminating poverty, their funds are spread evenly in over fifty countries of the world, though The Working World is more focused on the western hemisphere, including the United States (see their respective websites for 2015). Thus it may be that worker organizations must combine across borders to achieve the type of consideration they need. In any case, the MNER's historically more ideological and internationalist approach (as compared to the MNFRT's more legislative approach) has resulted in an essentially passive response from the Kirchner governments. As a comparative study indicated, 'In the final analysis, even new kinds of global conferences on new global issues with new global participants remain partially imprisoned by traditional roles and priorities in international politics. State sovereignty sets limits of global civil society' (Clark et al. 1998: 35). The meetings in Caracas under the Chávez government support the assessment of Susan Burgerman:

> Networks of activists operate across political systems irrespective of their nationality, occupying a political space that ignores the boundaries between states: they infiltrate governments and intergovernmental bureaucracies; they attempt, with varying degrees of success, to engage in the arena of international politics, formerly considered the sole preserve of states; they are simultaneous insiders and outsiders. As insiders, they are citizens whose political voice may be based entirely on resources provided by international allies. As outsiders, they are politically active non-citizens who stay involved over a period of time, still identified with international sources of power who become built into the political institutions of the country. (Burgerman 1998: 923)

Keck and Sikkink write of the boomerang pattern:

> When a government violates or refuses to recognize rights, individuals and domestic groups often have no recourse within domestic political or judicial arenas. They may seek international connections finally to express their concerns ... Domestic NGOs bypass their state and directly search out international allies to try to bring pressure on their states from outside ... On other issues where governments are inaccessible or deaf to groups

whose claim may nonetheless resonate elsewhere, international contacts can amplify the demands of domestic groups, pry open space for new issues, and then echo back these demands into the domestic arena. (Keck and Sikkink 1998: 12–13)

Cooperatives, civil society and the state

Argentina seems to combine the dual characteristics of Italian civil society as described by Robert Putnam. Within the same metropolitan regional context of the capital city, greater Buenos Aires, and the province of Buenos Aires, where over one third of the entire Argentine population resides, one finds in close proximity both elements of the Italian north and the Italian south as depicted by Putnam (Putnam 1993). On the one hand, we observe a rich melange of associational life with high union density, multiparty proliferation and high levels of participatory cultural outlets, while not many kilometers away one sees clear strongholds of elitism, verticality, religiosity, political clientelism and party patronage. The worker cooperative movements have been active within these cross-cultural geographies, and through their various capabilities have mounted a certain challenge to the Argentine political, economic and legal systems. Though they have come away with some victories and some defeats, they have managed to combine certain features that allow one to perceive them as proponents of 'contentious politics,' as social movements. Sidney Tarrow has provided a useful definition:

Contentious politics occurs when ordinary people, often in league with more influential citizens, join forces in confrontation with elites, authorities, and opponents ... They contend through known repertoires of contention and expand them by creating innovations at their margins. When backed by dense social networks and galvanized by culturally resonant, action-oriented symbols, contentious politics leads to sustained interaction with opponents. The result is the social movement. (Tarrow 1998: 2)

Certainly, Argentine worker cooperatives fulfill Tarrow's criteria for a social movement in that they use collective action because they 'lack access to institutions [and act] in the name of new or unaccepted claims, and ... behave in ways that fundamentally challenge others or authorities [while they build] organizations, elaborate ideologies, and socialize and mobilize constituencies, and their members engage in self-development and the construction of collective identities' (ibid.: 3).

It is important to remember that while the Argentine worker cooperatives, whether one considers them as several parallel worker cooperative economic alternatives, an extended network of recuperated factories and enterprises or a bona fide social movement, are but a small segment within the larger Argentine civil society, they do represent the challenges facing the whole gamut of the working class writ large now and in the future, representing at least 80 percent of the Argentine population. They offer a critique of capitalism's modus operandi. Though a part of extant civil society, they do not render obeisance to the ideology of the capitalist workplace hierarchy. Yet, as Michael Walzer has written, smaller civil society entities, such as worker cooperatives, eventually need to be sustained and protected against powerful and abusive employers, managers, and political party and trade union bureaucrats by a just state linked to that same civil society (Walzer 1998: 139). In a larger measure, as Gramsci wrote, the working people had to achieve independence from bourgeois political culture. 'Workers [and peasants] had to do more than simply join organizations, such as trade unions, that represent their interests; they needed to educate themselves, to learn to look at the structure of the state from their own perspective, and to develop the capacity to imagine a different kind of society and the collective will to struggle for it' (Buttigieg 2005: 23). In their essential forms they reflect once again Marx's notion of working-class freedom in which he argued, 'the associated producers, rationally regulating their interchange with Nature, bringing it under their common control, instead of being ruled by it as by the blind forces of Nature; and achieving this with the least expenditure of energy and under conditions most favorable to, and worthy of, their human nature' (Marx 1967c: 820; see also Marx 1983 [1844]: 131–46; Lukács 1971 [1922]: 27).

Granted, there is a fine line between worker organizations such as the MNER, MNFRT and later aggregations such as FACTA and CNCT qualifying as viable grassroots domestic networks and then blossoming into fully fledged social movements. To qualify as a successful social movement, according to Michael Edwards, they should have 'a powerful idea, ideal or policy agenda; effective communications strategies to get these ideas into politics, government and the media; and a strong constituency or social base that provides the muscle required to make those targets listen and ensure that constituency views are accurately represented' (Edwards 2004: 34). Should the worker-occupied factories and enterprises accumulate strength and resources, their potential egalitarian organization of the workplace can begin to have an effect on the democratization of the Argentine body politic. The multiplication of societal activism after the civil outbreak of 2001 brought the cooperative movement into a public forum predisposed to entertaining and promoting the needs of worker autonomy and control. Charles Tilly reminds us of the impact of social movements on democracy and democracy on social movements: Can social movements that are formed to pursue particular interests actually promote expansion of democratic relations and practices? (Tilly 2004: 140–43). On the ground Tilly sees most of the movements pushing very particularistic goals: 'Blocking construction of a highway, supporting abortion, forwarding the rights of indigenous people, and demanding better schools by social movement performances certainly take advantage of democratic liberties, but they do not necessarily advance democracy' (ibid.: 142). This is a very jaundiced and restrictive view of the viability of social movement activism that seems predicated on arguing for democratic outcomes only in retrospect rather than seeing the process as an ongoing struggle for access and legitimacy. Given the democratic nature of the cooperative workplace organization and the accumulation of multiple support bases among many societal reference groups, our answer to Tilly's question is a clear yes.

Once the worker-occupied factories and enterprises accumulate strength and resources, their egalitarian organization in the workplace can have an impact on the democratization of the body politic. The multiplication of societal activism after the civil outbreak of 2001 brought the cooperative movement into a public forum predisposed to entertaining and promoting the needs of worker autonomy and control. With the passage of individual temporary expropriation laws in various Argentine provinces and in the municipality of Buenos Aires, the legitimacy of the cooperative movement in the eyes of the public points in the direction of an accumulation of resources and support. Certainly, international moral support for the cooperative movement in Argentina has been forthcoming. Some of this advocacy can be laid at the doorstep of the promotion and international success of the 2003 documentary film *The Take* (*La Toma*), directed and written by Avi Lewis and Naomi Klein. The movie made the rounds of European and North American theaters and at world social forums, university and union hall screenings. It depicted the struggles of three factories as they achieved either municipal (Brukman) or provincial (Forja San Martín and Zanón) expropriation. Moreover, in December 2004, in just several days an online petition, sponsored by Lewis and Klein, directed to then president Néstor Kirchner and Neuquén governor Jorge Sobisch, called for the removal of threats of eviction and for the recognition of Zanón as a workers' cooperative. In just three days, 2,500 signatures were garnered from people all over the world. Again in November 2005, another petition directed to President Kirchner was circulated on the internet, calling for definitive expropriation of the Hotel Bauen Cooperative in the city of Buenos Aires. Again within three days, 2,700 people had signed. Another successful international petition on behalf of the Bauen Cooperative occurred in April 2014, responding to the last judicial eviction notice. In addition, a number of Argentine film collectives made video presentations both in Argentina and abroad as fund-raising and consciousness-raising mechanisms on behalf of the Argentine recuperated enterprises (interview with Argentine film-maker Cecilia Sainz, 21 July 2005). In April 2009 two Argentine cinematic producers, Virna Molina and Ernesto Ardito, presented a film in New York City and elsewhere depicting the conflictual history of the Zanón cooperative, entitled *El Corazón de la Fábrica*.

In conclusion: prospects for Argentine cooperatives

There is no absolute guarantee that the meaningful and realistic goals of these associations of workers will reach optimal fulfillment. Argentina, though it qualifies as a substantially vibrant civil society in most respects, has not shown a profound aptitude or willingness to confront the multiple obstacles to equity and fairness for those most in need. Civil society strength does not assure a level playing field, as is clear even in such an associational democracy as the United States. In a sense the proliferation of Argentine civil society works against the recuperating factories and enterprises and worker cooperatives. It allows the political and legal institutions with the power to promote their interests to treat these organizations with benign neglect. Rather than subsidizing a major national cooperative enterprise initiative to take its place alongside the large-scale and multinational corporations in Argentina, civil society as an amalgam has often tolerated a policy that forces the worker cooperatives to survive in a competitive climate in which they are thrown essentially on their own resources.

There are definitely serious obstacles to the long-term viability of the Argentine cooperative movement. The cooperative associations and their engagement with economic development draw attention to an important debate concerning the structural and decisional power of the state to effect dramatic changes in reorienting a country's resources on behalf of those in need. Argentine cooperatives, as part of civil society, act in areas that have not directly competed with or challenged state political and economic power. At the same time, the poor and the unemployed workers are given the space to rely upon their own political, organizational and entrepreneurial skills to survive in the neoliberal economy.

The Argentine worker cooperatives have drawn attention to major lacunae in the political economy of neoliberalism. Without significant and substantial support from the major institutions of government they have managed to etch out an area of economic survival that attests to alternative means of worker initiative, collective engagement and reconfiguration of the workplace. This has been no mean achievement. In striving to defend their families' livelihood, they have found themselves in ever-increasing confrontational relationships with capital, the state and the judicial establishment. As the workers proceed in the occupation and recuperation of their workplaces, they will be touching on fundamental questions concerning the direction of the neoliberal economy. As long as the worker cooperative movement accounts for a relatively small percentage of national production the confrontations will remain provincial and local. Thus far capitalist interests have prevented the use of essential and consistent credit opportunities for worker enterprises. Should the recuperation of factories and enterprises continue unabated, should it reach larger-scale economic entities, capitalist interests may begin to feel threatened and the potential for class confrontation may increase. This will require a re-examination of the role of the Argentine state rooted in a self-limiting vision of its responsibility for national economic development that affords work and social welfare for the whole population. Should a crisis of capitalism emerge, the workers' cooperative movement surely offers a systematic labor alternative. What's more, it may provide a model for a new cultural and ideological sea-change in working-class culture and consciousness.

The workers have convincingly argued that unemployment and poverty are likely to be continual companions of neoliberal capitalism unless worker-led enterprises are evaluated as formidable as well as alternative production models that deserve material and moral support. These examples of worker autonomy have demonstrated significant departures in terms of social formations. By their capacity to form alliances with progressive legal, community, political and labor forces available to them, they symbolize an alternative path to economic development that is predicated on worker solidarity and democracy in the workplace. The collective ownership of the workplace acts as a catalyst for worker creativity, ingenuity and sacrifice. In this the Argentine cooperative movement represents an intelligent, resourceful, micro-managed, pragmatic alternative to continued unemployment and poverty among the working class in Argentina. And in that cooperative approach to production, distribution and community outreach, they have created a meaningful and recognizable alternative to the hierarchical neoliberal capitalist organization of work.

Though Argentine cooperatives necessarily accept the market, they expect to offer a realistic confrontation to equity capitalism untied to community and country. They are interim economic associations of workers that, in the future, will offer new forms of societal engagements that challenge the *modus operandi* of the neoliberal capitalist economies.

7 | EMINENT DOMAIN: CONFRONTING THE LOSS OF JOBS IN THE UNITED STATES

Eminent domain and the solidarity economy

A serious crisis confronts the American working class unless public sector coalitions including social movements, community activists, labor, city councils and state legislatures band together to defend working-class jobs. Absolute capital mobility has to be challenged in the arena of legislation built on constitutional law. The right of expropriation is ensconced in the US Constitution. Eminent domain interventions are called for.

Plant closures have severe negative economic repercussions and impose societal externalities on workers and their communities. These economic fallouts then legitimize the right to regulate them by way of eminent domain on behalf of the public interest. Eminent domain legislation and application would create a public investment climate in manufacturing which has a clear multiplier impact on subsequently creating other service and commercial jobs, complementing the generation of industrial jobs. The impact on US economic growth and productivity would be clear. Beyond that, the growth of cooperatives represents efficient investments in job creations because the highly skewed salaries and compensations of owners and managers of equity firms are eliminated. The scenario of highly paid company executives demanding pay cuts and laying off workers would be eliminated.

The collective social rights of workers who have built up the value of the firm through years of hard work and applying their know-how and skill have to be legally asserted. The companies cannot be free of societal obligations. By outsourcing jobs they have broken a contract for which there must be reparations and consequences. Labor has few options, and the use of eminent domain can spark a public debate about the obligations of corporations and confront the passive acceptance of the steady decline of jobs with living wages.

Yes, there will inevitably be ebbs and flows in this struggle, contradictions and some setbacks and sidebars that redound to business interests. But the inevitability of the US loss of jobs and spreading poverty requires this kind of broad-based community coalition to challenge self-serving corporate capital. Today there are few alternatives under 'free trade' corporate initiatives, globalization of the workforce and international wage competition and advancing technological unemployment. Lumbering attempts to provide workers with social safety nets, portable health insurance or job retraining for displaced workers have not been achieved. We cannot expect labor to win the battle without a survival coalition that entails multiple urban mobilizations to defend employment in the US.

Workers are losing steady, high-paying jobs at an astounding rate with no effective response from organized labor. The productive infrastructure is disappearing at a breakneck pace as runaway firms search the world for cheaper labor, tax havens and developing-country governmental subsidies and lax labor and environmental protections. Even when these skilled US workers are able to find new employment, the majority fall to levels barely above the poverty line (Uchitelle 2006). Yet the American labor movement as well as American state and city politicians sit paralyzed before the decisions of corporate businesses which have benefited for years from state and local tax breaks and subsidies just for remaining in their present redoubts. But clearly they are not committed to their communities if the economic climate for profitability changes. In product after product, the US governmental entities have sanctioned downsizing and company rebirth offshore while neither labor nor state public officialdom has even begun to look for equitable solutions for the American workers threatened on a daily basis with loss of their livelihoods. Representative of this view was the position taken by President Bush's former chair of the Council of Economic Advisors, N. Gregory Mankiw, who said, 'outsourcing is just a new way of doing international trade' (*New York Times*, 11 February 2004; Mankiw and Swagel 2006). Former Federal Reserve chairman Ben S. Bernanke took virtually the same position, arguing that increasing US worker productivity even if it costs industrial jobs is to be welcomed (Bernanke 2006).

In what can be considered a landmark decision with great relevance for the struggling American working class, the US Supreme Court in *Kelo* v. *New London* (2005) ruled in favor of allowing New London by eminent domain to take over property for reasons of 'public purpose.' In conjunction with the previous construction by Pfizer Inc. of an adjacent corporate park and in an effort to rejuvenate a deteriorating section of New London, the city planning commission developed a commercial, residential and recreational project in a sweeping attempt at a broad development plan for an economically depressed city. The court ruled on behalf of New London's economic development plan based on the 'taking clause' of the US Constitution's Fifth Amendment, which states, '... nor shall private property be taken for public use, without just compensation.' Justice John Paul Stevens wrote for the majority that expropriation of private holdings as part of urban development is justified for the public purpose of increasing jobs and tax revenues. While *Kelo*, as well as previous uses of eminent domain, presents some risks as to whom it prejudices and whom it benefits, overall it can be seized upon as an opportune legal constitutional methodology. What *Kelo* offers is the defense of jobs as a key component of public sector responsibilities to communities.

In a previous relevant case, *Berman* v. *Parker* (1954), a unanimous court observed: 'The concept of the public welfare is broad and inclusive. The values it represents are ... physical, aesthetic as well as monetary.' Justice William O. Douglas wrote in part: 'It is within the power of the legislature to determine that the community should be beautiful as well as healthy, spacious as well as clean, well-balanced as well as carefully patrolled. In the present case, the Congress and its authorized agencies have made determinations that take into account a wide variety of values ... there is nothing in the Fifth Amendment that stands in the way.' It becomes clear in *Berman* that public use has been expanded to include 'public interest' and 'public welfare' by way of displacing 'blight' in a poverty-stricken neighborhood in Washington, DC. In still another case, the *Hawaii Housing Authority* v. *Midkiff* (1984), the state legislature transferred landownership from a few owners to multiple owners, again with just compensation, guided by the belief that restricting 'social and economic evils of a land oligopoly' qualified as a valid public use and a 'rational' effort to 'correct deficiencies in the market determined by the state legislature to be attributable to land oligopoly.' In essence *public use* has been substantially reinforced as *public purpose* as a more encompassing and functional interpretation of public policy responsive to the community as a whole, whether or not every individual has direct *use* of the facilities in question. This is eminently fair and realistic. When eminent domain is applied for the establishment of schools not all people will use them; similarly in the case of hospitals, libraries, roads, mass transit, parks, sports complexes and so on.

Kelo is just the latest Supreme Court finding that can be justifiably used by labor on behalf of the American working class. In this case it transferred to the City of New London and the New London Development Corporation the right to create a mixed industrial zone combined with a waterfront park and recreational area focused on creating new sources of employment while opening up a depressed, abandoned waterfront area to community access and enjoyment. Much of the *Kelo* backlash by private-property-owning interest groups fastened on the fact that Pfizer had to abandon its key place in the New London revitalization plans when caught up in the US recession beginning in 2007. Much has been made of *Kelo* and the negative impact of eminent domain in its use of state and municipal powers to transfer property rights from individual homeowners in poorer, marginal neighborhoods to larger private property enterprises that will achieve larger tax revenues.

Most eminent domain initiatives are not used to condemn mom-and-pop groceries or small homes for the sake of replacing them with larger operated business but rather with large urban, community mixed public and private complexes that provide increased employment, an enhanced tax base, urban development and community edification. As one legal observer indicated, 'When desperately poor urban communities are revitalized the vast majority of people in those neighborhoods benefit – the area is more beautiful and livable, jobs are more plentiful and inner city problems are curtailed. In *Kelo*, the city of New London was suffering from deep economic and social disadvantage, steep economic decline, high unemployment and fewer residents today than in 1920' (Goston 2006). The *Kelo* decision should focus American community groups and labor on activating municipal councils and state legislatures to promote a constitutionally affirmed right to expropriate factories and enterprises that have decapitalized their firms, fired workers and announced their plans to leave the US in search of cheaper wage labor and deeper tax concessions, leaving in their wake depressed American communities with ever-deepening unemployment and poverty.

Clearly, applying eminent domain to take over on behalf of its workers a factory or enterprise that has been left to founder because its owners have begun to move its machinery and equipment offshore or to a more welcoming economic environment within the United States is unique in and of itself. Its uses do not benefit in the least a private developer or interest but are applied for the public good of a group of workers which will redound to the general welfare of that community.

Eminent domain, via the Fifth Amendment's 'takings clause,' has been used in America for over 180 years. It is not an unusual measure. It requires the expropriation with compensation of private property for public benefit and has been considered an attribute at any level of independent sovereignty. It is clearly a part of the vision of the writers of the US Constitution that legislators have the right to expropriate property for a greater public purpose (Harrington 2002). In the early part of the nineteenth century, grist mills in New England were constitutionally allowed to dam up rivers that often flooded their upstream neighbors. It was defended by the courts on the grounds that these decisions redounded to the benefit of the general public consumption of processed corn and other grains. Before the adoption of the Fourteenth Amendment, the eminent domain provision of the Fifth Amendment did not necessarily apply to the states. By extending the rights of private property to all citizens, it also expanded the reach of what is intended by the greater public good. It has been applied by community groups to reclaim vacant properties for the purpose of housing and economic development. The Dudley Street Neighborhood Initiative lying between the Roxbury and Dorchester communities of Greater Boston, culminating in its success in 1988, is testament to the positive usages of eminent domain (Medoff and Sklar 1994). The initiative by Mayor Gayle McLaughlin and the City Council of Richmond, California, moves us in the right direction and provides a powerful test case of the potential uses of eminent domain. The Richmond plan intends to purchase underwater mortgages of homes in danger of foreclosure from the banks at the fair market value and return then to the homeowners and readjust their mortgages to their real market value. If the banks refuse, eminent domain will be applied to defend the economic integrity of the community and avoid the impact of blighted neighborhoods (Dewan 2013).

In fact, one could point to many other instances when the residue from the usages of eminent domain resulted in the increased potential of people of modest means to buy a home by dint of the general economic improvement of their community. It contradicts the argument that is often the crux of the legal defense against a community-supported renewal project. There are multiple examples of the power of eminent domain to revitalize neighborhoods, create jobs and provide an enhanced tax base. In cities and towns like Brooklyn, New York, Indianapolis, Indiana, Hartford, Connecticut, Kansas City, Kansas, Estes Park, Colorado, Thomson, Georgia, Canton, Mississippi, among others, eminent domain has proved crucial in creating and maintaining viable alternatives to deindustrialization, unemployment and poverty. In the *Kelo* case *amici curiae* briefs were presented by such eminent domain advocates as the Brooklyn United for Innovative Local Development, the National League of Cities, the National Conference of State Legislatures, the US Conference of Mayors, the Council of State Governments, the National Association of Counties, the International Municipal Lawyers Association and the International City/County Management Associations. Mayors such as Eddie Perez of Hartford, Connecticut, and Bart Peterson of Indianapolis, Indiana, also understood the importance of the *Kelo* decision and testified accordingly before the US House and Senate Judiciary Committees in September 2005.

Deindustrialization in America has become a fact of life since the mid-1970s and promises to continue as a rising tide without any alternative strategies from American labor unions. Ever since the failure to save the Youngstown Sheet and Tube Company, an Ohio steel mill, in 1977, industrial enterprises have found little to stop them from shifting their investments to developing countries in which labor costs, tax write-offs and other seductive entitlements provide the basis for much higher profit margins. In the Youngstown case, community folks wanted to contribute to making the plant a community property. The funds were insufficient to effect the buyout and local and national politicians were not amenable to subsidizing the venture with grants or loans (Safford 2004). As Barry Bluestone and Bennett Harrison noted a quarter of a century ago, a projected worker-owned factory like Youngstown needed a short-term public subsidy to support the venture or jobs could not be saved (Bluestone and Harrison 1982: 252ff.). In its absence, the preservation of enterprises and jobs is arduous if not impossible. At the time of the Youngstown closing, the steel workers went to court to try to save their plant but the judge in the case could not rule on their behalf without plant-closing legislation. He said in part, '... the Youngstown community cannot be dismissed as inconsequential. United States Steel should not be permitted to leave the Youngstown area devastated after drawing from the lifeblood of the community for so many years. Unfortunately, the mechanism to reach this ideal settlement, to recognize this new property right, is not now in existence in the code of laws of our nation' (Lynd 1981: 43–4). This is, of course, not accurate for Ohio or anywhere else. The US Constitution and various state constitutions would allow for such legal interventions if there is a groundswell demand for such policies. They are prescribed by law. What is missing is the willingness of states and municipalities to intervene with enterprise expropriations and subsidies for the workers facing the loss of their livelihoods.

In the last analysis, worker rights were subordinate to capital. Jack Beerman and Joseph Singer make the case well when they write,

> the struggle between employers and employees over job security is an example of the larger struggle over property rights in society in which owners are often allowed to exercise their rights without regard for the interest of others ... The argument over job security is, at bottom, an argument about morals, human dignity and the proper distribution of power in the workplace. (Beerman and Singer 1989: 951)

Legislation by way of eminent domain was and is called for, and it is a legal alternative awaiting use at the municipal and state levels.

In another significant and controversial case before the Michigan Supreme Court in 1981, *Poletown Neighborhood Council* v. *City of Detroit* has demonstrated the flexibility with which municipalities and courts understand city needs where economic development and jobs are concerned. Here a state supreme court allowed eminent domain for private use based on the understanding that the public would be an important beneficiary of industrial revitalization. In this case, the city of Detroit received an offer from General Motors (GM) to construct a 3-million-square-foot assembly plant at a cost of $500 million to replace an aging Cadillac assembly and Fisher Body plants that GM proposed closing in 1983. For Detroit, this provided an opportunity to retain over six thousand jobs that would otherwise have permanently been lost to that city if GM moved to a distant alternate site. Poletown, as a sector of the city that was deteriorating, offered significant unused space and was near the rail and highway transportation access required by GM. Detroit was willing to provide the 500 contiguous acres plus a twelve-year, 50 percent tax abatement. The community took its case to the Michigan Supreme Court, which held 5–2 on behalf of the city of Detroit. The court held that the project contained a 'public purpose' within statutes governing the general health, safety and welfare of the community, while alleviating unemployment, rehabilitating a blighted neighborhood and fostering economic development. The court argued that 'eminent domain could not be used without substantial proof that the public is primarily benefited.' It further argued that 'the controlling public purpose in taking this land is to create an industrial site which will be used to alleviate conditions of unemployment and fiscal distress. The fact that it will be conveyed to and ultimately used by a private manufacturer does not defeat this predominantly public purpose.' And the argument continued, 'There is no dispute about the law. All agree that condemnation for a private use or purpose is forbidden. Similarly condemnation for a private purpose cannot be authorized whatever its incidental public benefit and condemnation for a public purpose cannot be forbidden whatever its incidental private gain. The heart of the dispute is whether the proposed condemnation is for public or private use.' And the Michigan legislature had determined that this Detroit/GM initiative met a public need and served a public purpose. *Poletown* is significant in that it presents starkly the importance of political, community, labor and business interests coalescing around the use of eminent domain in the creation and defense of skilled jobs, the maintenance of an important tax base and protection against community decline.

Mayor Coleman Young's testimony at the time spelled out the implications for the Detroit community:

> I think it transcends in its economic and social potential for
> this community the renaissance or any other development that
> has taken place. What we have here is a development that is
> being watched by older industries in the Midwest and northeast

across the nation. If we can assemble this land, doing justice to those who live there, both the merchants and the residents, and provide a strengthened industrial base for our state, I think we can open up an approach for other northern industrial cities ...

Like *Kelo* later, *Poletown* had many detractors among private property advocates and those seeing eminent domain abuse. However, when deindustrialization becomes the core challenge to the survival of the American working class, public policy requires interventions that create some innocent victims but the larger goal of supporting majoritarian employment for at-risk communities becomes incontestable. And certainly when we speak of applying eminent domain as an existing methodology on behalf of worker-owned and worker-managed cooperatives, these kinds of objections do not carry weight. The arguments used against applying eminent domain on behalf of the working class lose all ethical, moral and material gravity. Using eminent domain on behalf of the US working class does not represent corporate gains of any kind nor does it represent small homeowners losing their property. Rather it represents groups of workers defending their place of employment and maintaining their lives in their communities.

8 | BUILDING TOWARD WORKER COOPERATIVES BY THE USE OF EMINENT DOMAIN IN THE UNITED STATES

Cooperatives and eminent domain as complementary organizations and processes

As the many Occupy movements in the US, from New York to Oakland, have shown, there is a global groundswell for democratic alternatives to oligarchic-controlled capitalist firms. It testifies to the yearning for more participatory means of existence. Workers themselves can similarly respond to capitalist employer decisions to close a plant, remove the machinery and break what is a social contract. Worker occupations are the necessary and required response to runaway companies, just as Occupy Wall Street (OWS) was to the financialization and corporatization of the American economy. Public opinion had cast a favorable eye on Occupy movements as they touched deep-seated needs among all sectors of society (*New York Times*, 26 October 2011). Worker cooperatives, however, have the organizational staying power and proven longevity that OWS was not able to achieve.

Where cooperatives have flourished, they represent a major challenge to public policy by not beginning with a generalized, diffuse left-critique of capitalism that does not have a clear and defined entry point. Rather, recuperated enterprise cooperatives, for example in Argentina, represent a challenge to employers that has a majoritarian basis because their working-class needs and demands are so reasonable yet comprehensive. They typify the real frustrations of the unemployed, the precariously employed and the underemployed and should receive the sympathy and support of most citizenry in any capitalist country.

The Occupy movements claimed legitimacy for the commons and public spaces (Harvey 2012). Workers have those same rights to claim their factory and workplaces, and those rights are even more specifically grounded in time and place. Occupy Wall Street represented an important breakthrough that demonstrated that we can indeed come together at crucial times as workers, social movements, community activists, students, academics and progressive labor unions (Ranis 2011). Workers have this right because they have already put in decades on the job when the owners claim bankruptcy or decide to downsize, outsource or abandon their community (Ranis 2007).

This is clearly the breach which working-class cooperatives can penetrate today, and they have done so in Spain, Argentina, France, Canada, the US, Greece and Venezuela, among many other countries (*Guardian Weekly*, 8 May 2015). The majority of the US working class find themselves not only in manufacturing but in the services, in commerce and among contingent workers, subcontracted workers and immigrant workers. All of these groups deserve the benefits and entitlements that capital–labor reorganization would provide for them. Workers need to embrace the knowledge that worker-owned and -managed workplaces are a realistic and grounded alternative.

The US has more than three hundred worker cooperatives, some startups and others partially subsidized by city councils in, for example, New York City and Madison, Wisconsin. They represent not only industrial plants but such diverse enterprises as engineering, architecture, computer technology, bakeries, house cleaning, assisted home care and construction. California, New York and Massachusetts combine to house over one third of the cooperatives (Nzinga Ifateyo 2014). In New York City the inspirational driving force emanated from the Federation of Protestant Welfare Agencies (FPWA). In its groundbreaking study, *Worker Cooperatives for New York City: A Vision for Addressing Income Inequality* (2014), it laid out the need for cooperative development as a response to growing inequality, joblessness and the plight of low-wage workers. Using its connections with the New York City Council it helped sponsor a hearing in which over fifty cooperative owner-workers, community and academic advocates (including this writer) testified before the council's Committee on Community Development in early 2014. These exchanges resulted in a June 2014 New York City Council allocation of $1.2 million for the further support and incubation of New York City cooperatives. Again, in June 2015, the New York City Council appropriated another $2.1 million to further its Worker Cooperative Business Development Initiative, which would seed the creation of an additional twenty-two new worker cooperatives in New York City to join the already existing twenty-two and employ a projected additional 300 worker-owners. In Madison, Wisconsin, $5 million will be devoted to cooperative development over five years beginning in 2016. In Madison Mayor Paul Soglin and the Madison Common Council were apprised of the New York City cooperative initiative and felt that its local traditions allowed for at least the same type of cooperative commitment (Nzinga Ifateyo 2015).

Yet as promising as these new increasingly concerned understandings of the need for municipalities to address the support of startup cooperatives are, state governments, by and large, fail to heed these concerns. Whereas cooperatives have to force their way into conversations to achieve a hearing for their plans for economic development to enhance employment in metropolitan areas, it remains patently clear that private corporations have the ear of state governments when they seek subsidies and tax breaks to maintain their economic footholds. Their arguments are comparable to those of defenders of cooperatives, but their clout is larger as they demand state support in order to avoid closing their business or avoiding bankruptcy. A good example of this policy, which excludes cooperative support while subsidizing corporate threats to leave a community and impact on its unemployment rolls, occurred in New York State in November 2015. To maintain an Alcoa plant in the community of Massena, New York, Governor Andrew Cuomo has committed a subsidy of $70 million to avoid the aluminum company from closing or relocating abroad (McKinley 2015). Compare that expenditure for one upstate company to the New York City Council's subsidies of $3.3 million for forty-four cooperatives in the equally depressed and needy areas of New York City.

In Chapters 3 and 7 we described the need to develop cooperatives and the available uses of eminent domain to further these alternatives to hierarchical capitalist enterprises. As indicated, the US has the legal mechanism provided by the US Constitution and the state constitutions that would allow for the initiation and establishment of worker-owned and worker-managed cooperatives emanating from the 'takings clause' of the US Constitution. The Fifth Amendment clause states: '… nor shall private property be taken for public use, without just compensation.' Eminent domain is thus legally sanctioned and has been applied multiple times for community, infrastructure and development purposes. Eminent domain allows for the municipal or state governmental expropriation with compensation of enterprises in default or which threaten to leave a community and its stricken workers for reasons of maximizing equity profits.

Preserving working-class jobs and maintaining community health and welfare clearly fall within this concept. Civil society's need must take precedent over the sanctity of private property. The writings of William Blackstone, legal philosopher and jurist in eighteenth-century England, gave credence to state obligations over John Locke's seventeenth-century view of the preeminence of the absolute right of private property (Locke 1960 [1690]; Blackstone 2014 [1766]). Blackstone argued that state sovereignty had important responsibilities that took precedence over private interests. The Brandeis Brief (1908) stimulated judicial decisions that began to acknowledge the worth of social science and public testimony. Later, as Associate Justice, Louis Brandeis argued that the rights of property have to be remolded from time to time to meet the changing needs of society. His decisions drew upon extralegal data and evidence to support his arguments (Urofsky 2009).

Various Supreme Court cases (e.g. *Berman*, 1954; *Midkiff*, 1984; *Kelo* 2005) have been decided on the basis of the use of eminent domain for public use and/or public purpose. In addition, there are various state cases such as *Poletown* v. *City of Detroit* (1981) and various private transportation and utility proceedings in Minneapolis (1974), New York City (1976), Wisconsin (1978) and Connecticut (1982) – all strengthening the use of the takings clause of the Constitution for a greater public purpose, be it for ending community blight, correcting inequitable usage of land, economic development, employment or providing for a public need.

Once expropriated, the factories and enterprises would then be turned over to the workers themselves, who have the technical skills and know-how to run these industries. In Argentina, for example, workers have shown they can maintain and manage enterprises and industries, be they metal plants, tire factories, food processors, chemical plants, meat packing plants, textile factories, auto parts installations, electronic component suppliers, ceramic factories, lumber plants, glass factories, supermarkets, printers and publishers, health clinics, hospitals, or hotels and restaurants, as successful and viable establishments (Ranis 2014).

Using eminent domain

There are two principal stumbling blocks to the use of eminent domain in the US and elsewhere: a) the underlying ideology of the sanctity of private property and b) the understandable but misguided willingness of workers to accept severance pay and walk away from their jobs. These impediments can be counteracted by political education of both the general public and policy-makers by organized movements, community activists, academics, public intellectuals and progressive labor unions.

It is only since the advent of Reaganomics that we have had John Locke's ideas again being promoted via the Institute of Justice (1991), a right-wing think tank, and the Castle Coalition (2002), a right-wing advocacy group, which have fastened on 'eminent domain abuse' as a term of opprobrium which muddies the waters of its potential positive uses and outcomes.

The processes of creating cooperatives from runaway enterprises will not be an easy road but once negotiated successfully will provide a recognizable default methodology that will redound and reverberate in multiple settings nationwide. For example:

1. Workers, on learning that their factory or enterprise is about to move, close or claim bankruptcy, must occupy the facilities. This is paramount. Without this first step, the rights of workers to achieve fairness and justice will usually be given short shrift, not be recognized or even considered. It will just be the case of another factory or enterprise closing down.

2. Workers must gather the support of the surrounding community – this prospect has been made considerably easier since the Occupy movements began in 2011 in many major US cities such as New York, Chicago, Oakland and elsewhere. A groundswell of support is a necessary ingredient in achieving the 'righteous indignation' that workers deserve and will get for being deprived of their livelihood and the community losing a contributor to its health, welfare and societal comity.

3. A workers' cooperative must be organized, demonstrating the workers' labor history and potential viability and longevity within the departing firm. Establishing a cooperative is not a difficult process and each state has clear stipulations on accomplishing the legal reorganization of the enterprise.

4. Public sector intervention by way of the legal tool of eminent domain must be applied by local city councils and/or state legislatures. By and large, workers usually do not have the financial wherewithal to purchase the exiting enterprise. What is of great importance is that the workers are occupying and reorganizing a company or enterprise that has clear assets that are recognizable and worthy of being fully restored to the workers.

5. Finally, in most cases, after the application of eminent domain, it will be necessary to grant a short-term public subsidy or low-interest public seed loans to the workers or, in some cases, allow the workers to attain the funds from non-profit funding sources that enable them to buy out the runaway enterprise. State and municipal public subsidies and tax breaks for industries and real estate builders are very common within the US states. The same financial response needs to be made for protecting jobs, enhancing tax rolls and preventing community decay with accompanying unemployment and resulting poverty. In any case, it is a public investment that will redound to the community in multiple ways. For their survival, the workers have an intrinsic commitment to repay any public loans made on their behalf.

Why eminent domain?

As we have argued in Chapter 7, factory and enterprise closings have severe negative economic repercussions and impose societal externalities on workers and communities. These economic fallouts legitimize the right to regulate them by way of eminent domain on behalf of the public interest. Eminent domain proceedings require due compensation to the firm at market valuation at the time that the firm has declared bankruptcy or is about to resettle elsewhere in the US or abroad.

The collective social rights of workers who have contributed to their community through years of hard work and applying their know-how have to be legally asserted. The companies cannot be free of societal obligations. By outsourcing jobs they have broken a social contract for which there must be consequences. State and municipalities must recognize that the public interest has been subverted and that the formation of cooperatives fills the void left by the departing enterprise.

We need to use eminent domain for development purposes much as we use the legislative rights to tax and spend, zone for economic purposes, and regulate for consumer and environmental protections.

In the US, eminent domain has been used for many decades for building highways, airports, hospitals, municipal offices, libraries, public parks and sport complexes, in the name of urban and community development and the public benefit. It is especially appropriate to apply this same rationale to protect against the loss of the industrial and service jobs of the US working class (Ranis 2007). We need to use eminent domain for development purposes much as we use taxation, regulatory and zoning legislation. What greater public purpose could there be than preserving employment for the same public that represents 99 percent of society?

When workers occupy factories and enterprises they are not really *taking* something. They are trying to *keep* something that is already theirs, through their work, through their production of important goods and services, through allowing capital to be invested, and supplying the community with their taxes, their consumption expenditures and their everyday involvement in the civic life of their community.

In defense of the working class

Worker ownership and management of the workplace are clear alternatives to hierarchical owner companies in benefiting community economic development, social justice and worker autonomy. Otherwise we condemn these workplaces and the surrounding communities to unemployment, a shrinking tax base, poverty and the erosion of the skilled labor force. We have a legal mechanism that will place worker rights at the center of the political debate. Using eminent domain on behalf of establishing worker cooperatives creates a defense against deindustrialization and working-class unemployment and will preserve both factory and service jobs in America.

While *Kelo*, as well as previous uses of eminent domain, presents some risks as to whom it prejudices and whom it benefits, it clearly can and must be seized upon as an opportune legal and constitutional intervention on behalf of the US working class. The eminent domain concept should be embraced by organized labor, public sector interests and civil society groups committed to socially redeeming activism that redounds on behalf of the weakened and challenged American workforce. What *Kelo* offers is the defense of jobs as a key component of public sector responsibilities to communities.

Kelo and other court case findings can be imaginatively used by communities on behalf of the American working class. In the case of *Kelo* it transferred to the City of New London and the New London Development Corporation the right to create a mixed industrial zone combined with a waterfront park and recreational area focused on creating new sources of employment while opening up a depressed, abandoned waterfront area to community access and enjoyment. The recession of 2007 and beyond undercut the plan severely as it did much damage to economic development throughout the US. But the intent was correct and valuable as a precedent in using socially worthy public policy initiatives by way of eminent domain.

Runaway companies, without significant penalties or repercussion, leave hundreds of thousands of workers and their respective towns and cities and move their investments, assets and equipment abroad, accentuating unemployment, devastating communities and undermining the industrial infrastructure of the US. In almost all cases of runaway companies, they search out other venues whether in the US itself or abroad not because they are losing revenue or are near bankruptcy but because they simply choose to earn even higher profit margins elsewhere regardless of the consequences to their labor force.

Although there are thousands of credit, consumer, housing, utility, insurance and agricultural cooperatives in the US servicing millions of Americans, there are only about three hundred small worker cooperatives in which workers are truly involved in day-to-day organization and participation in production and services. The use of eminent domain can provide the impetus to bring such worker-owned and-managed enterprises into the critical discussion about recovering jobs in America.

Legally, eminent domain can legitimize the worker-owned and worker-managed factories as they strive to maintain their jobs and salvage the enterprises for themselves and their communities, while organizing for the larger goal of defending industrial and enterprise development and viable employment within the US. We have seen examples of worker comprehension of their rights as the creators of capital and their rights to keep their industry and jobs when equity firms have sought to vacate the premises and break contracts with both workers and communities. We have the inspiring examples of the Republic Windows and Doors workers in Chicago in 2008/09 and again in 2012, the Stella D'Oro bakery workers in the Bronx, New York, in 2008/09 and the Taunton, MA, Haskon Aerospace workers in 2010/11 taking the crucial initial steps of sit-down strikes and factory occupations to oppose equity firms leaving the workers and communities in their wake. In each of these cases equity firms Gillman, Brynwood and Esterline have removed equipment to cheaper sites in other states or other countries. The latter two plants have closed, throwing 136 and 100 workers into unemployment, and in the Chicago case a new firm had taken ownership (Serious Materials) and had rehired only a small percentage of the 260 former workers. Again, the new firm planned to shut down its facilities in 2012. This time the workers, by dint of examples they had garnered from Argentina, shifted their strategy to ask for time to raise the funding to purchase the factory and establish a workers' cooperative. In this they had the critical financial and logistical support of The Working World, a non-profit, micro-lending organization, and the United Electrical Workers local union, and were able to establish the New Era Cooperative.

Factory occupations, sit-ins and petitioning public authorities to save jobs are the necessary backdrops to advocacy for the application of eminent domain procedures. The formation of worker cooperatives by US working-class and middle-class employees has major potential if supported by labor unions and central and municipal labor councils combined with community organizers and activists. Desperate times call for desperate measures, and factory and enterprise occupations need to be placed on the immediate horizon. American labor unions, by and large, have acquiesced by simply focusing on slowing down employment contract givebacks. They have bargained with corporate owners under the rules of the game that severely limit and undermine the rights of the workers. In this regressive scenario, the only way for the working class to have autonomy is if they run the factory or enterprise themselves, as opposed to endless worsening collective bargaining contracts. Workers must initiate eminent domain proceedings in every single case of a runaway ownership, and it must become the de rigueur default initiative everywhere in the US so that it becomes a reflexive, multiplier process accepted as a legitimate legal response to arbitrary and irresponsible behavior by private owners.

The American public has shown in surveys that it supports tax increases to bridge budget deficits rather than decreasing pay and benefits to the working class or reducing healthcare, educational expenditure or public transportation (*New York Times*, 1 March 2011). There is little question that public opinion would support workers defending their jobs and homes against equity firms whose commitment is not to any particular community or country but to themselves and their investors. Similarly, in recent public opinion surveys in Argentina, 86 percent of respondents supported workers' rights to recuperate factories that were about to close, the vast majority answering that the workers are defending their workplace, which is a product of their past labor, and 97 percent gave recuperating enterprises a positive evaluation (IIGG-CEDESAL survey, 2012). These responses offer great hope that as cooperatives proliferate they will increasingly gather community support and cooperation. Chains of worker cooperatives could then become regional interlacing industrial zones committed to each other's existence and survival with an outreach to ever wider communities in terms of educational, cultural and job opportunities. We see this kind of municipal support and cooperation in the Cleveland green, interlinked worker cooperative network, which includes hydroponic greenhouses anchored by the Cleveland Clinic and Case Western Reserve University (Alperovitz 2013).

Worker self-empowerment in the US: beyond factory occupations

After occupying the factory or enterprise, it is critical to take the second step by forming a worker-managed cooperative enterprise and calling for city or state legal action using eminent domain. Leaving the factory before securing political and legal support, as happened in the case of the courageous and defiant Stella D'Oro bakery workers on strike in the Bronx, New York, in 2008/09, is not the best alternative. The 136 workers had shown themselves to be a coherent and solid group, striking for eleven months to resist draconian job givebacks. Not a single worker crossed the picket line, while they engaged an important but small community, political and labor support group and used Local 50 of the Bakery Confectionary, Tobacco Workers and Grain Millers (BCTGM) union to obtain a positive National Labor Relations Board (NLRB) ruling that mandated back pay and benefits. Almost immediately after the NLRB ruling in July 2009, Brynwood Partners, the equity firm that now owned Stella D`Oro, announced plans to close the factory and eventually sold it to the manufacturer Lance, Inc., which moved the company to Ohio in the fall of 2009.

As important as the Stella D'Oro solidarity outreach had been it was not enough to save the jobs of the 136 workers. Without a decisive plant occupation, community groups and a smattering of labor union activists alone are not enough to carry the day. Labor union rank and file are often far too mute observers of capital offenses against the working class and rarely act beyond their own immediate role as individuals within society. They await trade union leadership to speak for them, and that is most often simply unavailable. Concerted worker activism from below is the required first step, followed by the use of eminent domain proceedings instituted by the municipalities involved. Forming worker-managed cooperatives must become the final aim. In New York City neither the city council nor the mayor provided the necessary critical support. Had OWS been in place at that time, there is little doubt that this movement could have provided the necessary community mobilization on behalf of these Bronx workers.

In Taunton, MA, workers, again of the United Electrical Workers (UE), were in a serious labor conflict with Esterline Technologies, which planned to move 100 jobs to non-union plants in California and Mexico. The Taunton plant, Haskon Inc., made door sealants and silicon gaskets for aircraft. Despite being a profitable enterprise with profits of $120 million in 2010, Esterline announced it would auction off the equipment in December 2010 to pay for the workers' severance package. The UE was able to get the support of Congressman Barney Frank, state legislators and the city council to request a delay of the auctioning of the Haskon equipment until mid-February 2011. For the first time in recent modern labor history, the union then attempted to initiate eminent domain proceedings, with the support of the Taunton City Council and the mayor, to seize the Esterline machinery and buy the property and factory on behalf of the workers. According to the Massachusetts Constitution's law of home rule, eminent domain can be applied to taking of property, both personal and intangible (machinery and equipment).

This purposeful and creative approach sadly failed for several reasons. First, the Taunton City Council in late December 2010 passed a home rule petition sent to the Massachusetts legislature to apply the use of eminent domain to purchase the company machinery and equipment. A home rule petition became a necessary procedure because Esterline did not own the building, only the machinery and equipment. Second, the Esterline Company demanded $300,000 for the equipment and machinery from the Haskon workers to avoid an auction that would probably yield a third of that. Third, the auction occurred on 19 January 2011, two days before the Massachusetts legislature would reconvene to even consider an eminent domain intervention and, in the interim, the severance package was approved by the aerospace workers at Haskon.

This labor confrontation in Taunton, MA, demonstrated the possibility of applying eminent domain to runaway plants. The UE and the workers were able to get the support of local unions, the Jobs with Justice Chapter, the Massachusetts Nurses Association, the Jewish Labor Committee, the Greater South East Massachusetts Central Labor Council and community residents of Taunton. They were able to use this groundswell to get the city council and mayor to vote in favor of eminent domain and to get voices of support from state legislators as well as their congressional representative, Barney Frank. As in the Stella D'Oro case in the Bronx, New York, an important factor was the certainty of a severance package as opposed to the challenges of the struggle, both political and financial, to see eminent domain proceedings to their conclusion. This requires a good deal of courage on the part of the workers involved, as well as the willingness to depart from the norms of previous plant-closing scenarios. Unless eminent domain becomes a manageable choice, a default alternative, severance payouts will continue to poorly compensate workers while closing their industries and commerce throughout America.

The UE Chicago workers took that first principled and reasonable step of peacefully occupying and maintaining the Republic plant ready for production. This resonated as a powerful message and an opportunity for the American working class to make that cultural leap (Ness 2011: 318). In February 2009 a bankruptcy court judge ruled that a California building materials company (Serious

Materials) could purchase the plant's assets and employ the 260 workers involved in the occupation of the factory (Lydersen 2009). However, this alternative was fraught with the uncertainty of market calculations undertaken by the private buyer. By mid-2010, Serious Materials had rehired only thirty workers. Again it would have been appropriate if a progressive community and political coalition in Chicago had called for intervention from the city council to implement eminent domain proceedings.

Nevertheless, the Republic workers have learned an important historical lesson that represents a change in the political climate in the US. After those six heroic days of occupation by most of the 260 workers of the plant, and significant support from local, state and national politicians, including President Barack Obama, the owners relented via a newly stipulated loan from Bank of America, which had just been bailed out by the federal government to the tune of $25 billion. Eventually a buyer was found from California called Serious Energy (formerly Serious Materials), which promised to rehire all the workers as they resumed production. Three years later only about a third of the workers had been rehired.

By late February 2012, the new owners again announced an immediate illegal shutdown. Again the workers occupied the plant, asking for time to come up with a plan to find a new buyer or establish a worker-managed cooperative plant. This time, because of the groundswell of community support for the plant, led by Occupy Chicago and Jobs with Justice, instead of taking six days, it took but eleven hours for the workers of Republic Windows to be given a three-month reprieve, which was subsequently extended. Dramatically, in May 2013, the workers established the New Era Windows Cooperative, the largest industrial worker cooperative in the US. One of the leaders of the workers, Armando Robles, spoke of plant occupations and worker cooperatives created in Argentina as their model. The sacrifice in this Chicago cooperative was *sui generis*, since workers had to raise their own substantial capital of $665,000, with the crucial help of The Working World, and move, on their own, piece by piece, the equipment and furnishings to a more economically sustainable location in the same Chicago area. Nevertheless, it provides a model for recuperating workplaces in the US that have been destroyed by owners seeking higher profit margins elsewhere. In that regard, in January 2016 the New Era

Windows Cooperative workers finally received a $295,000 payout in a bankruptcy court for the violations of the NLRB act, which requires two weeks' notice before a plant closes (Lydersen 2016). Robles hoped that their struggle through occupation would become something repeated across the US and the world when workers face similar arbitrary closings. Another leader of the New Era Windows Cooperative, Ricky Macklin, said, 'In opening up this plant we have learned we are so much more than what we thought we were. In opening up this plant we've done our own electrical work, we've done the plumbing work. And all we thought was we were just window makers' (GRITtv.org, 9 May 2013).

Final comments

In essence, cooperatives and recuperated enterprises are in the last analysis defensive strategies that allow the workers to act 'as a class in itself and for itself,' as Marx advocated. These structures combine human values of self-interest and survival with real democratic participatory life. On the other hand, liberal democratic representational government is not in the workers' personal ken, nor has it proved over time to be worth their commitment and struggles. As the Occupy movements have shown us once again, one must combine economic self-interest and knowledge with actual on-the-ground democratic participatory life. In taking over the factories and enterprises, workers can concretize the Occupy movements and act as essentially confrontational agents that represent themselves and, in so doing, represent the overwhelming majority of people in any given community. When workers occupy a factory or enterprise they are reasserting their significant place in their community.

In this strategy, it is crucial to expand the narrow definition of private property. Whose property is it anyway? That of the erstwhile owners and managers who accumulated the original capital and initiated the investment proposal or that of the workers and employees who have made the enterprise a working reality through years and often decades of commitment and hard work? Workers cannot be separated from the capital they have produced. A necessary collective contract has developed over time that makes the workers and employees responsible in the final analysis. This relationship (effectively a social contract) has superseded the simplistic notion of private property as belonging to the owner.

Worker-managed factories and enterprises represent an attempt to bypass and even subvert the traditional capitalist firm as they experiment with workplace organization that avoids the top-down controls of the capitalist hierarchical firms. They plant the seed in acknowledged market economies that there is another way of organizing work. Eminent domain should not be considered a revolutionary policy departure. It conforms to traditional regulatory legislative public policy that includes the powers to tax and spend, to regulate places of work environmentally, to zone for economic purposes, to apply rent control and to protect employees and laborers and the surrounding community from health and safety hazards. Worker control simply requires a more novel approach that uses eminent domain on behalf of workers for the clear benefit of economic development, social justice and worker autonomy. Otherwise we condemn these workplaces and their surrounding communities to unemployment, a shrinking tax base and working-class poverty, with the concomitant rise of Medicaid, early use of inadequate social security benefits and the continuing erosion of America's skilled labor force. One can only surmise the impact of not turning to eminent domain procedures. It requires recalling the consistent subtext of Marx's later writings in which he demonstrates capitalism's dependence on unemployment and a reserve army of the unemployed for its longevity (Jameson 2011).

How can communities continue to stand idly by while crucial employers, who have fed from the public trough and their loyal workers, often for decades, decide to get up and leave when the eminent domain procedure is available? Eminent domain remains the untapped viable legal mechanism that will place worker rights at the center of the political debate in the defense against the continuing decline of decent jobs in North America, and reactivate what Marx considered a major advance within capitalism itself: the free association of worker producers.

9 | CUBAN COOPERATIVES AS A
GATEWAY TO ECONOMIC DEMOCRACY

After fifty-five years of mutual antagonism, the establishment of dip-
lomatic relations between Cuba and the US in December 2014 and
the opening of the US embassy in Havana in August 2015 provide a
significant opportunity for Cuba to experiment with adopting market
practices and/or using the end of direct hostilities to focus on its own
potential to deepen and expand its forms of participatory socialism.
The end of the paternalistic Soviet ties in 1990, after almost thirty
years, created a cathartic decline in the Cuban economy from which
it is still in the process of recovering. It is important to remember
that the Cuban socialist revolution survived the fall of Soviet and
eastern European communist systems and continues to attempt to
find its own way toward a just and effective society and economy.
Cuba represented a heroic struggle to survive that precipitous fallout
and dramatic decline in its economy, and has continually looked in
the last two decades for the ways and means to defend its revolution
without betraying its historical commitments. In that context, the
biggest challenge for the future of Cuban participatory socialism is
how to integrate and adapt the new initiatives of the US begun under
the Obama administration. The Cuban political leadership has to
decipher which US initiatives have value for the Cuban people and
which are meant to undermine the Cuban version of socialism.

Cooperative-based socialism is the most hopeful initiative to
come out of the 313 articles in the new 2011 6th Communist Party
Congress's *Economic and Social Policy Guidelines for the Party and the
Revolution* (*Proyecto de Lineamientos de la Política Económica y Social por
El Partido y la Revolución* – hereafter, the *Lineamientos*/Guidelines).

The new *Lineamientos*/Guidelines' preamble speaks of 'from each
according to his/her capacity to each according to his/her work.' This
reiterates the Marxian concept, put forward in Karl Marx's 1875
Critique of the Gotha Program, that under socialism this is required
as it builds toward a future communist society that indeed can
achieve the principle of 'from each according to his ability to each

according to his needs!' The *Lineamientos*/Guidelines go on to say: 'The recommended economic policy guided by the principle that socialism is about equal rights and opportunities for all citizens, rather than egalitarianism. Work is a right and a duty, as well as a source of motivation for every citizen's self-accomplishment, and must be remunerated in accordance to quantity and quality.' Early in the document it spells out the need for new approaches necessary for the reform of the Cuban economy. Immediately after the focus on foreign investment comes the mention of the new initiatives advancing cooperative developments in Cuba. The document restates the irreversibility of Cuban socialism but stresses the critical need to eliminate its fiscal deficit and improve its balance of payments, promoting economic efficiency through labor motivation, import substitution policies in agriculture and industry and the increasing production of high-value-added production.

The *Lineamientos* (Guidelines proposals nos 25–9) directed specifically at cooperatives focus on voluntary organizing that brings together resources and labor to produce goods and services for society while assuming all costs and profits achieved. The 2011 Guidelines were followed on 15 November 2012 by Decree Law 305 (Gaceta Oficial de la República de Cuba 2012), the most explicit governmental support for cooperatives ever produced anywhere in the world. It demonstrates the Cuban government's fully fledged commitment to making worker cooperatives a crucial part of the continuing Cuban socialist revolution.

Though they are still considered an experimental economic initiative, it is clear that the Cuban government considers cooperatives an essential part of Cuba's approach to fostering economic development while at the same time maintaining the integrity of the Cuban socialist revolution. The focus on non-agricultural cooperatives in the new law makes clear the intent to universalize cooperatives within the whole service and industrial economy. The Cuban opening to cooperatives follows closely the seven cooperative principles of the International Cooperative Alliance (ICA). The Cuban decree-law of 2012 speaks of the 1) voluntary and free association of its members; 2) the cooperation and mutual support of its members; 3) the democratic nature of its collective decision-making; 4) cooperatives having the autonomy to distribute income proportionate to the workers' contributions after meeting their tax obligations; 5) members' commitment to the aims of the cooperatives; 6) the responsibility of the members to contribute to the planned development of the Cuban economy, to the welfare of the cooperative's members and their families, to the protection of the environment and to promoting its activities without speculation; and 7) collaborating and cooperating with other cooperatives and state entities by way of contracts, agreements and lawful activities. Their charter is in line with global cooperative principles and commitments to voluntary, participatory and democratic cooperative procedures.

The law promotes inter-association among more than one cooperative as a way to complement and supplement economic activities that produce value-added economies that have multiplier impacts, such as the buying and selling of their collective products and services. What is unique in the Cuban cooperative model is that cooperatives formed by spinoffs from state enterprises have a lease arrangement rather than out-and-out ownership, though the leases can be renewed for twenty years. Other independently formed cooperatives can make offers to lease properties from state institutions.

On the other hand, the relevant Cuban bureaucracies are very slow in giving approval to newly forming cooperatives and procedures are laborious, winding their way from hearings at municipality level to approval from the national Standing Committee for Implementation and Development (Comisión Permanente para la Implementación y Desarrollo) and finally presentation to the national Council of Ministers.

As in most cooperative structures elsewhere, each cooperative has a president, a vice-president and a secretary voted on by the whole assembly of workers. Up to twenty members, a cooperative can elect an administrator, from twenty to seventy members an administrative council, can be elected and with over seventy members the workers can elect a board of directors as well as an administrative council. Cuban cooperatives can contract non-cooperative salaried workers for up to three months to carry out functions that the membership cannot assume, though these contracts can never exceed 10 percent of the workers in the cooperative. After the three months, the contracted workers can solicit to be accepted as full members or be let go.

The move to form cooperatives has been well received by the Cuban working class and many are attempting to receive approval for new, more profession-specific ventures such as groups of language specialists, booksellers, ornithologists, information technologists, economists, engineers, lawyers, accountants and translators. The field of cooperatives has been appended to university courses and plans are afoot to include it in secondary and primary school curriculums as well (López and Buffa 2015). An auto repair and body and fender mechanic speaks of his new cooperative experience:

> It's different. Everything is changing. You are the boss, you create everything, you work for yourself, for your family and you don't depend on a company but rather on yourself. Your family on seeing your progress wants to join the cooperative which makes it more like a family because they see the results and want to join this venture. (Ibid.)

However, compared to the new self-employment initiatives already under way, these proposals will take much more time and planning. The governmental self-employment initiative *Cuentapropistas* has targeted 181 activities but, given the socialist orientation of the Cuban government, will be closely regulated by licensing fees and substantial taxation. Nevertheless, it allows entrepreneurs to hire employees, to hold multiple licenses and to sell to government entities, state enterprises and joint ventures (Peters 2015: 150). However, the government is taking a clear position that is both progressive and defensive when it comes to the development of the self-employed sector. It is intent on preventing the growth of large capitalist enterprises by applying a progressive tax on the use of employing wage labor. The self-employed *cuentapropistas* can hire up to five workers exempt from taxes, but a tax of approximately $18 (450 Cuban pesos [CUPs]) a month for hiring six to ten employees, $40 (1,000 CUPs) for eleven to fifteen employees and $7 (175 CUPs) a month for each additional employee is added. In addition, personal income is taxed progressively. Net annual personal income of $400 is taxed at 15 percent, $400 to $800 at 20 percent, $800 to $1200 at 30 percent, $1,200 to $2,000 at 40 percent and over $2,000 in net income at 50 percent. Thus it appears that a fundamental objective of Cuban tax policies is to control the size of companies, preventing a concentration of assets in private hands (Pons Pérez 2015b).

Since the 1968 prohibition of all self-employment, Cuba has

slowly begun to allow such endeavors over stages since 1979, with a rapid rise by 1994 because of the Cuban economic crisis caused by the post-Soviet economic decline and, since 2010, a public policy that has endorsed their expansion (Díaz Fernandez 2015).

Cuba's cooperative initiatives provide an alternative reform to Cuba's state socialism while, at the same time, presenting a policy option that would thwart a new capitalist ethic to overwhelm the state, which continues to be committed to preserving basic societal needs in food, housing, education and health. As of 2014, Cuba, according to the United Nations Development Program (UNDP), ranks 67th of 188 nations, below Argentina, Chile and Uruguay but ahead of such countries as Brazil, Mexico, Venezuela, Colombia and Costa Rica in the Human Development Index. This index measures such areas as life expectancy, healthcare, educational levels and gross national product per capita (UN 2015).

Cuba, certainly since the advent of Raúl Castro in 2007, has been seeking to unleash an incentive system, and loosen party and state controls without becoming another developing capitalist system. Though it appears that Cuba is directing its attention to the Chinese and Vietnamese models, there is no clear sense that this is definitive. The outlook is further complicated by the influence of Spanish, Italian, Canadian and, of late, US relationships conforming to some of the tenets of liberal capitalism, putting Cuba into dependency relationships with capitalist trading partners, especially given the more than uncertain future of Venezuelan commitments. The US, recently exploring the investment opportunities in Cuba, has relaxed the rules for allowing companies to open locations in Cuba and hire Cuban workers, facilitating financial transactions between the two nations. In October 2015, US Secretary of Commerce Penny Pritzker traveled to Cuba, the first Commerce Secretary to visit Cuba since 1950. It has become patently clear to US businesses that American capital has arrived late in terms of foreign investments. For example, the deep-water container port of Mariel was financed by Brazilian capital, operates with Chinese equipment and is managed by a Singapore firm (Hirschfeld Davis 2015b).

A new Cuban investment law promulgated in March 2014 creates a scenario that gives foreign enterprise a predominant role at the port of Mariel. The Cuban view is that the foreign investment initiative is absolutely crucial if economic growth is to take precedence, and economic growth is a prerequisite if subsequent structural reforms are to follow (Figueras 2015). The investment law provides strong incentives for foreign capital from such countries as China, Russia, Spain and Canada. Taxes on foreign profits have been dramatically cut in half and new foreign investors receive tax exemptions for the first eight years. In addition there will be no taxes on foreign companies' imports and exports. Finally foreign subsidiaries can be wholly owned as against previous arrangements in which Cuba maintained 51:49 percent control (Hirschfeld Davis 2015a). These tax benefits and incentives condition the Cuban economy toward a capitalist orientation that makes cooperative development an ever more critical and essential departure if democratic socialism is to remain a viable endeavor.

In 2014 the Cuban agricultural sector represented 20 percent of those employed but contributed less than 5 percent to national income (Díaz 2015). What may have begun as simply a need to make the woefully underproductive Cuban agricultural economy productive again by severely reducing the *Acopio*, the giant state farm product-purchasing enterprise system, has been transformed into a series of much broader-based economic reforms. These initiatives have expanded cooperatives more universally as means not only of enhancing a new mixed public–private economic model but of setting in motion an explosion of pent-up urban initiatives geared to satisfying the first necessities of everyday consumer needs. The self-employed workers, the worker cooperatives and the small-scale businesses that provided a real product or a real service are no longer seen as the enemy of socialism; rather they are seen as the drivers of the engine of development. Moreover, such workers could convert themselves into something distinct and qualitatively more efficient than Cuba's historical wage workers. They could reflect a new type of social actor as a free associated worker (Campos Santos 2012a: 1–3). The minimum wage in Cuba is $12 a month, while the typical Cuban wage workers are paid very low, if not miserable, wages in Cuban pesos (CUPs), while many desired goods are available only in Cuban Convertible Pesos (CUCs) equivalent to US dollars, each CUC being worth 24 CUPs. In 2014, 25 percent of 11.2 million Cubans lived in poverty (Gonzáles 2015). Cooperatives could mitigate these conditions and improve markedly the situation of the Cuban working class simply in the area of their incentives to work and produce and the improvement of their basic purchasing power.

Since the US trade embargo of 1961, later including all financial transactions (1963) and the implementation of the Cuban Assets Control Regulations (CACR) and Department of Commerce regulations, everything to do with travel and commercial relations was strictly monitored. Subsequently, the Helms-Burton Act (1996) created multiple onerous conditions placed on Cuba's economy and society before the lifting of the embargo. Under the Obama presidency travel and remittances were restored for Cuban families (2009). In 2012, it was estimated that over 400,000 tourists arrived from the US, the great majority Cubans living in the States. Further travel restrictions were lifted in January 2014, which allowed Cuban-American families to travel to Cuba without Treasury Department approval, as well as the use of US credit and debit cards in Cuba when issuing companies establish themselves in the country. By 2015, the CACR had eased travel restrictions for such visitors to Cuba as journalists and educational, academic and professional researchers (Sullivan 2015). In early 2016, the US's CACR was amended further to remove financing restrictions for authorized exports, and US banks could provide credit for those exports (Havana Times 2016). Most important for the development of the private sector in Cuba was approval for the expansion of exports of goods and services to the Cuban entrepreneurial sectors in such critical resources as building equipment and materials for private sector residential construction and farmers' equipment needs.

These policy changes, plus the loosening of remittances to Cuba, may have the impact of heightening economic inequalities in Cuba that benefit those with relatives and friends in the US and creating more visible class differences in Cuba, redounding most negatively on the Afro-Cuban population with fewer connections to the US mainland. On my way to Cuba in the summer of 2013, I witnessed the long lines of Cuban-Americans at Miami airport, with literally tons of items such as televisions, CD players, freezers and other household goods, which, for the Cuban recipients of these products, had huge economic multiplier impacts within Cuba. It is also suggested that remittances from the US go mostly to the informal economy (Nova González and González-Corso 2015). Thus those Cubans with access to the import of goods by way of family and friends in the US are able to sell them in the free market price at the US-equivalent CUC price for a considerable profit (Ritter 2013: 38). That would certainly accentuate class differences since these money inputs do not target the formal working class with fixed and poor incomes.

It is easy to forget the important achievements of the Cuban Revolution between 1960 and 1970, which laid the basis of a society committed to egalitarian social policies – massive land distributions to small farmers, reduced urban rents, minimally priced medicines, the almost total elimination of illiteracy and unemployment and the nationalization of exploitative foreign enterprise holdings in companies, banks, mines, sugar plantations and refineries. The history of the Fidel and Guevara leadership and policies has often been acknowledged as an excellent teaching example of what a socialist society must do to promote its methods and protect its ideals. And yet almost twenty years of replicating the Soviet model undermined the Cuban culture of autonomy and creativity. Only since the 'special period' has Cuba again needed to find its own way to socialism. Compared to the Soviet model, Cuba has always had higher degrees of popular mobilization via the Committees for the Defense of the Revolution (CDRs), the Organs of Popular Power, the women's federations (FMCs) and the University Student Federation (FEU), which always gave Cuba a special feel, despite the impact of the Cuban Communist Party (PCC) taking precedence by the mid-1970s and the beginnings of Soviet influence via intermittent party congresses.

By 2015, 498 cooperatives, of which 416 are in the service sector (70 percent), had been approved by the government; 385 are conversions from formerly owned state enterprises and 114 are from individual group proposals. Sixty-three percent of the non-agricultural cooperatives have been formed in the province of Havana and the two new neighboring provinces of Artemisa and Mayabeque (Font and Jancsics 2015; Díaz Fernandez, 2015). The vast majority (83 percent) of the cooperatives being formed are in the areas of retail food services, gastronomy, restaurants, coffee bars and catering (49 percent), commercialization through farmers' markets (20 percent) and construction (14 percent) (Vuotto 2015: 18–19). Despite these initiatives, Archibald Ritter writes that cooperatives still employ less than 5 percent of the Cuban working-age population, compared to

21 percent in the private sector and 74 percent in the public and state sectors (Ritter 2016).

Nevertheless, one estimate predicts that by 2016 3,000 cooperatives will have been initiated, the vast majority in the restaurant and gastronomic fields (Pérez Villanueva 2015a). Though the non-state sector comprising entrepreneurial initiatives and cooperative formations represents but 7 percent of GDP, the Cuban state is clearly committed to this expansion (Fernández Aballí 2015; Gershon and Lippman 2015). At this time most of the non-agricultural cooperative development remains in the services which require fewer scarce resources, more available human capital and an immediate profit margin.

By 2011, Cuba had 217,000 cooperative members and 147,000 *cuentapropistas*. In addition it counted more than 100,000 new private lease-holding farmers that have emerged since 2008 (Piñeiro Harnecker 2013b: 51). However, the cooperative sector remains very small when compared to the immense growth of the private sector, made up of 477,000 largely micro businesses, or compared to the impact of the much larger 6,000 or so state enterprises (Fernández Aballí 2015). Among those so self-employed, 68 percent were not previously employed, 14 percent were formerly retirees and 18 percent were part-time self-employed since they also worked in the state sector (González Corso 2015), 26 percent were women and 32 percent were young people (Díaz Fernandez 2015). These data obviously point to a dramatic unleashing of formerly underemployed and now productive sources of economic productivity. Another possible motive in Cuba for the unleashing of both the cooperative and *cuentapropista* sectors is the extent of the underground, informal economy of people (1.3 million) who are not employed in the formal sector, not studying at a secondary school or university and not actively looking for work (Fernández 2015). To bring entrepreneurs in from the black market, licenses have been granted to those without *vincula laboral* (with no current workplace) (Peters 2015: 149).

As in the US and elsewhere, cooperative formations can keep the Cuban rural inhabitants from moving to urban areas in search of jobs in the service and tourist sectors (Sosa 2015). This would qualify as a substantial measure for engaging a potentially alienated labor force. Cooperatives, from a socially responsible perspective, also act as an alternative to self-employment in that the likelihood of tax evasion is minimized because of the greater solidarity commitment of cooperative members. However, as elsewhere, forming cooperatives creates greater challenges than simply working on one's own as a self-employed *cuentapropista*. Many members of the working class are used to taking directions from state enterprise employers and receiving a salary. These are relationships often difficult to supersede in inaugurating a cooperative (Barrera Rodríguez 2015). Vuotto also documents, in her detailed study of the Cuban cooperatives, the still-remaining challenges of fulfilling the many regulatory steps prior to certification, the lack of available investment income and access to sources of wholesale supplies (Vuotto 2015: 25).

Cuba is potentially trying to establish greater working-class hegemony by weakening the role of the state sector and essentially unleashing the productivity of civil society. On the other hand, it is not entirely evident whether a working-class consciousness has sufficiently penetrated the political culture to bring this off. It isn't clear whether the Cuban Revolution hasn't been an example of Gramsci's 'passive revolution' using the Cuban working class all these years as a mobilizational force without giving them real power, and now unleashing civil society's productive capacity but without giving the working class an input into influencing the direction of the state. That was certainly my impression on my trip to Cuba in 1973 under the auspices of the New York City-based Center for Cuban Studies. The Cuban state socialist evolution harkens back to the Soviet example in which revolutionary change on behalf of workers' greater control in workplaces did not occur because it was not well incorporated during the early stages of the Soviet political process (Wallis 2011: 15–16).

In Cuba we find a groundswell developing on the edges of a society still basically dominated by party, state and enterprise bureaucracies. The recent Communist Party Guidelines/*Lineamientos* of April 2011 point to a recognition that the political system must adapt to the potential efficacy of working-class productivity and empowerment. In fact, there is much criticism in Cuban society that the very open and participatory party congress that led to the Guidelines did not sufficiently acknowledge the concerns of many of the delegates' interventions concerning the loosening up of the political system, the role of unions and of worker decision-making in the workplace (Hernández 2015: 87). In April 2016, the 7th Party Congress meets, and here again it will be important to see whether the cooperative initiatives in the Guidelines of 2011 are given sufficient priority to compete with the expanding private sector. This party congress is possibly the most important congress in Cuban socialist history in terms of how cooperatives will fare in the new economy.

The long period of dependence upon the Soviet model of centralization is undergoing severe criticisms from both the progressive left and more traditional liberal economists in Cuba. It is the beginning of an acute self-criticism reminiscent of the internal critiques of the Soviet Union and the Eastern bloc of writers like Leon Trotsky (1972 [1937]), Milovan Djilas (1957) and Miklós Haraszti (1978). It has become clear to many within the Cuban intelligentsia that state ownership of the means of production is a far cry from worker ownership and control, nor is it a prescription for rapid economic development. Cooperative development even had the early support of Lenin in his belief that cooperatives were necessary if the Soviet state was to achieve socialism. What it required was a cultural revolution of participation by the population that would enhance and complement the dominance of the state (Lenin 1965 [1923]). Intellectuals on the Cuban left fear a potential developing alliance between European and US corporate capital and a form of Cuban state capitalism (Campos Santos 2015; Ocaña Díaz 2016).

A very thorough analysis of the current Cuban political and economic context comes from Armando Chaguaceda. He astutely evaluates the continuing challenges to Cuba building a democratic socialism. He writes in part,

> The Cuban state has demonstrated its role as the defender of national sovereignty, sponsor of development, and guarantor of social justice through the redistribution of goods and services. But it has also proved its inability to satisfy a great number of Cuban society's expectations for participation, with its vertical model of development, in which top management positions in the state and in the Communist Party overlap and are occupied by the so-called historical leadership (i.e. Fidel Castro's generation of leadership). At the lower levels, there is usually a similar overlap among party leaders serving as government leaders; this is particularly visible in the provinces and the countryside ...
> Without such participation, institutional performance

has been symptomatically precarious, as centralization, administrative discretion, and personalism, from national bodies to local ones, have put a halt on collective dynamism and deliberation. In this system of organizing collective life, social spaces, whether organized or informal, tend to be subsumed or simply controlled by the state within an asymmetrical power structure ...

Since 2007, the government has employed classic administrative and technocratic solutions including installing new officials to oversee other officials and shrinking the bureaucracy. But there has been no effort to expand citizen participation based either on the socialist traditions of bottom-up collectivities (workers' councils, self-managed businesses, and popular assemblies) or on contemporary democratic innovations that continue to emerge in many parts of Latin America ... In preparation for the Communist Party's various congresses, the state has sponsored National Debates that call for a broad discussion of national issues and prioritize consultative forms of participation, but they are territorially fragmented and thematically parochial.

Participation, as it is defined in practice, has a consultative bias in the sense that citizens' discussions take place on courses of action that have already been outlined and determined at higher institutional levels, such as the Council of State and the Politburo ... Policy corrections are exclusively up to the leadership, which operates with total discretion. This has been the experience in the debates ahead of party congresses (1991and 2010). (Chaguaceda 2015: 112)

This analysis is echoed even more powerfully by Julio César Guanche, when he writes of the high marks he gives for Cuban political participation but mediocre marks for actual political representation of demands from society. He cites the Cuban election system, which does not allow local political campaigns to debate candidate issue differences. And he sees the political system as deficient in that the National Assembly delegates do not act as representatives of the society at large but rather of the state and the Communist Party before that same society. He argues that the leadership, while seeking opinions, criticisms and suggestions, still controls the actual decision-making. The National Assembly legislator, rather than representing his/her constituency, is more likely an adjunct of the state, resolving problems within society as a whole. Policies and directives go from the top down and the lower echelons are expected to follow and contribute to them. Finally, Guanche argues that Cuba's highly participatory society has the mass organizations, citizen groupings and political spaces to construct a more collectivist democratic socialism (Guanche 2012).

Fernando Ravsberg argues that in the four decades since the Cuban Constitution was promulgated there has never been a legislator in the National Assembly who has voted against a governmental law, decree-law or resolution. He adds there is much discussion among the 600 men and women legislators but in the final analysis the legislation is unanimously approved. This is so because more than 90 percent of legislators are subject to the discipline exercised by their Communist Party affiliation (Ravsberg 2012). Solar Cabrales agrees, and writes that this lack of authentic political input has resulted in political passivity and the atrophying of critical judgement from below (Solar Cabrales 2012). And Campos Santos argues that without direct elections for national, provincial and municipal offices, candidates will not truly represent their constituencies. Under present conditions, the Communist Party still exercises overwhelming weight on who is nominated all the way up to the National Assembly (Campos Santos 2012b).

Another danger lurking is the abandoning of the greatest proponents of the Cuban Revolution that this author has observed in various trips to Cuba between 1990 and 2013, and compared to my first trip in 1973 (Ranis 1976). The focus on economic reforms and entrepreneurial support leaves behind those on fixed income public sector jobs, teachers, academics, professionals and those who have been among the most fervent and committed supporters of the revolution. At the same time it often unleashes people who have been passive opponents of the socialist revolution and even its enemies. Taxi drivers and pizza venders earn more than school teachers and professors moonlight as taxi drivers. Another sector that will be challenged are those seniors who are fired from governmental posts but are no longer able to adapt to the new economic rules of the game. Pensions for public sector retirees are approximately $10 a month, hardly sufficient to provide for their needs (Nova González 2012). In 2010, 1.9 million Cubans (17.4 percent) were over sixty years of age (Pérez Villanueva 2015b:

141), and just in the year 2011 500,000 state workers needed to be relocated (ibid.: 140; Peters 2015: 148).

The expropriation process required in Latin America and the use of eminent domain in the United States will be unnecessary in Cuba, but the implementation of cooperatives will follow similar procedures as workers begin to organize themselves into collectively and democratically run enterprises separate from day-to-day state interventions. Cooperative developments in Cuba will have a much better chance of flourishing given the more predictable access to public financing, technical assistance, wholesale material purchasing and governmental contracts.

However, the state presumptions and rationale are similar: workers must be afforded greater autonomy and decision-making in order to be more productive and less alienated. The Cuban state seems to have decided that cooperatives are 1) both rational in that they will keep the laborers and employees in productive jobs and avoid the unemployment, extreme social poverty and malaise that is dangerous to the Cuban state during its economic transition, and 2) the right thing to do by way of enhanced income levels and income distribution, and by way of collective associations, after years of repressed consumer demands for the majoritarian working class in Cuban society.

The Cuban moves toward worker cooperatives are one of the means to democratize, debureaucratize and decentralize Cuban society and politics. Much criticism has been leveled at the fusion of political power and subordination to the Communist Party, the state apparatus and the 'Revolution' as an expected hegemonic commitment. It seems clear that the Cuban Workers' Federation (CTC – Central de Trabajadores de Cuba) has been since its creation a governmental and party organ, intent more on conveying public policy mandates and stimulating productivity than representing worker rank-and-file grievances. The focus on private self-employment and cooperatives has also become a priority because of the overdependence on government employment, which represents 80 percent of the Cuban workforce, and the service sector, which constitutes 81 percent of GDP (Nova González 2012).

The Cuban private sector employment of 15.7 percent has been largely concentrated in the agricultural sector of independent farmers in the Credit and Service Cooperatives (CCS – Cooperativas de Créditos y Servicios), founded in the 1960s. Then there are the Agricultural Production Cooperatives (CPA – Cooperativas de Producción Agropecuarias) developed since the 1970s, when independent farmers volunteered to aggregate their holdings into larger productive units in return for subsidized new housing and cultural and entertainment improvements. These pioneering groups anticipate the current cooperative movement in the countryside and represent the DNA of today's cooperatives. Lastly, the Basic Units of Cooperative Production (UBPC – Unidades Básicas de Producción Cooperativas), introduced during the 'special period' crisis in 1993, have proved much less successful because of their lack of autonomy and dependence on state production and distribution controls (Nova González 2012). In 2014, 923 UBPC cooperatives showed profits of $2,697,000, while 249 of these cooperatives showed losses of over $10 million (Vuotto 2015: 11). According to Nova González, the CCS and private farmers (National Association of Small Farmers – ANAP) prior to 2010 generated 57 percent of food production on only 24.4 percent of the cultivated land so that the new governmental initiatives have provided the CCS and private farmers with 35.8 percent of such lands to increase production (Nova González 2013: 84–5). By 2014, the CCS alone produced 75 percent of Cuban vegetables while holding only 18 percent of the land (Vuotto 2015: 12).

Thus, historically, Cuba has already experimented with agricultural cooperatives. But their administration remained essentially top-down without the clear autonomy of the farm workers themselves. In June 2008, Cuban society learned that less than half of available agricultural land was being cultivated (Diaz 2012: 3)! This became the clear opening impetus in creating new forms of economic activation. Under Raúl Castro's government's Decree-Law 259 in 2008 nearly 15 percent of agricultural land was distributed in usufruct to private farmers and existing cooperatives (ibid.: 3–4). Longer usufruct rights of ten years have been legalized since October 2012 in order to provide a greater sense of continuity and security of the farmers' holdings. Much of the farmland had been underutilized and it is estimated that 80 percent of agricultural products that are imported currently could be grown in Cuba (Nova González 2012).

With the passage of Decree-Law 300 in December 2012 more hectares are now available in usufruct so that 1½ million hectares have been distributed to 172,000 Cubans and approximately 83 percent of the agricultural land is now in the hands of a variety of cooperatives of varying degrees of autonomy (Diaz 2013).

The Guidelines/*Lineamientos* of April 2011 devoted several sections of the 313 proposals to the formation of cooperatives in Cuba. When speaking of 'decentralization' it was clear that cooperative formation was one such alternative promotion. Under general management reforms of the economy, cooperatives are mentioned along with the self-employed sector, the liberal usufruct expansion in the agricultural sector and the mixed capital–state enterprises. These are all essentially new, legitimized departures for Cuba's socialist society. It becomes clear from reading the Guidelines that a new emphasis on self-management is being advanced as opposed to top-down centralized mandates from the party and/or the state apparatus. Sections 25 to 29 of the Guidelines are devoted exclusively to the development of worker cooperatives, not only grade 1 individual cooperatives but, if they so evolve, also the creation of grade 2 cooperative federations that would achieve greater worker solidarity and efficiency.

On 11 December 2012, the Cuban government initiated a period of cooperative development presaged by the Guidelines of 2011. Cuba is the first socialist state to fully embrace the formation of worker cooperatives. The constitutional cooperative reforms have been approved at the highest levels of the Cuban government. Hence it appears as a thoughtful and well-planned series of measures. The law was sanctioned by not only the Council of State and the Council of Ministers but also the influential ministries of Financing and Prices, and Economics and Planning.

It is envisioned that there will be industrial, service and commercial urban cooperatives formed in 222 non-agricultural economic areas such as transport, gastronomy, domestic and personal services, raw-material recovery and production and construction services. The cooperatives are to be run by worker assemblies with each worker having one vote and deciding on its administrators from within.

With the approval of petitions submitted to the local municipal governments (*Poder Popular*), the cooperatives can be initiated by either combining the assets of members or by renting the property or other fixed assets from the government. Cooperatives are given ten-year leases and rental priorities, including one year's free rental and a lower tax rate when compared to the self-employed sector.

A further difference in operation from the self-employed sector is that cooperatives may hire temporary workers for only ninety days before admitting them to full cooperative membership or ending the relationship. Lastly, cooperatives will be given preferential credit options from the state as well as raw materials at wholesale prices as opposed to retail prices. All these indicators point to a substantial and committed move by the Cuban government to launch a serious and determined cooperative economic sector based on both democratic and productive principles.

The cooperative development in Cuba is congruent with the need to increase Cuban economic productivity, which has never fully recovered from the fall of its Soviet and eastern European suppliers and subsidizers. Cuba's recent focus on non-agricultural cooperative development is geared to an import substitution policy that would focus first and foremost on providing sufficient foodstuffs for its own population and eventually initiating industrial cooperatives as well.

The economic openings in Cuba are dramatic. Self-employed enterprises with hired labor can access credit and rent facilities from state enterprises. At the same time cooperatives are forming in non-agricultural service sectors and permitted to develop commercial relations with the booming hotel and restaurant establishments. The state enterprises are being decentralized and made more autonomous in an effort to shrink government ministries. Local provincial and municipal governments are being chartered to levy their own taxes and decide on economic investments. Another powerful motor for economic stimulation has been the freeing of sales of both houses and automobiles without institutional regulations (Pérez Villanueva et al. 2012). Overall, the decentralization of the Cuban economy appears to parallel the needs of Cuban provinces and enhance the proliferation of cooperative formations guided by the needs of people in local communities. These are continual challenges to the centralized cultural traditions of the Cuban socialist state.

It seems increasingly clear that Cuban professionals, since the release of the 2011 Guidelines, have been encouraged to think strategically, even if these approaches represent significant departures from past economic practices. There is much discussion in Cuba not only concerning cooperatives but also the formation of mixed and co-administered enterprises, as well as municipal and communal economic entities. Economists in particular have the ears of departmental ministries. For example, members of the Center for the Study of the Cuban Economy (CEEC) hold dozens of regularly scheduled meetings with governmental ministries and state enterprise officials on the optimum means of implementing the party economic Guidelines (interview, Betsy Anaya 20 June 2013).

On the other hand, the left critique of Cuban state socialism does not have the ear of the government but represents an insistent resistance to both returning to corporate capitalism and the continuation of socialist blueprints inspired by party congresses from above without worker participation. Pedro Campos Santos, one of the more prolific critics within Cuba, takes this approach. He has argued that neither the Cuban state nor large private capital can fulfill the needs of wage workers. In both cases, the salaried working class lacks the power to control the means of production – the key to self-empowerment. This requires rather that organizing begin from below, allowing workers to create productive organizations of self-management. According to Campos Santos, the only way to do this is through the spread of cooperative enterprises and private entrepreneurial initiatives. This could then lead to a democratic participatory society at large (Campos Santos 2016a). Apparently, Campos Santos does not fear the *cuentapropista* sector of the Cuban economy developing into large capital holdings. In any case, for the first time in living Cuban memory the focus for Cuba's travails has shifted from the undoubted burdens of the US embargo to domestic deficiencies as the principal source of economic stagnation.

The Cuban '*libreta*' – the ration book for heavily subsidized basic food products – will probably be very slowly phased out for the general population while remaining for the truly needy. It cannot yet be superseded until Cuba's dual currency is unified. But as yet the dollarized convertible CUC currency cannot fully replace the national peso currency because the economy is not yet productive enough and the limited supplies and commodities keep the prices far too high for the Cuban population. Some basic goods such as gasoline, cooking oil, chicken and beef products, detergent, toothpaste and toilet paper are controlled by state sales monopolies that make their distribution in CUCs to the typical consumer problematic (Campos Santos 2016b). In the interim, the ration book will remain the order of the day. And, of course, subsidized public services, free public health and education and low utility (97 percent subsidized) and transportation costs (bus ride at about 2 US cents) are thus far untouchable hallmarks of the Cuban Revolution. In 2014, 50 percent of the national budget was still devoted to education and health expenditures (Pons Pérez 2015a). Such governmental programs make Cuba unique in the developing-world economies.

In addition, there is a massive redistribution of labor from layoffs in the public sector, and the push for self-employment and cooperative experiments in services, commerce and light industries such as food processing, transportation, construction, cafeterias, restaurants, barber shops, beauty parlors and home repairs (Piñeiro Harnecker 2013a 4). It was expected that by 2015 employment in the non-state sector would embrace almost two million Cubans or 35 percent of those employed (Pérez Villanueva 2013: 34; Piñeiro Harnecker 2011: 69), and that 1.8 million Cubans would have been dismissed from the state bureaucracies (Mesa-Lago 2012). This expulsion will certainly add another economic uncertainty, creating a large new 'reserve army of labor' available for exploitation in the new self-employed entrepreneurial sector. Cuban cooperatives can fill that breach and avoid such fallouts.

Conclusion

Creating Cuban cooperatives as an essential component of the ongoing Cuban socialist revolution is a goal that can become a momentous initiative on the part of the political leadership. I recall the very important speech by Fidel Castro to Cuban intellectuals at the Cultural Council shortly after the Bay of Pigs victory in June 1961, when the Cuban revolutionary leaders felt an encouraging solidarity and confident about the future. In a speech dedicated to opening the literacy campaign on behalf of vast swaths of rural people locked in the Cuban countryside, Castro also warned that intellectuals and artists must avoid stances outside the confines of the socialist revolution. It was the prelude to a congress of intellectuals that would form the Union of Writers and Artists (UNEAC). In his monumental presentation, which would set the boundaries of the Cuban Revolution, Castro made clear to succeeding generations the vision and limits of cultural, intellectual and political departures that would be acceptable to the Cuban leadership cadre. In complex and subtle language, Fidel argued that intellectuals must be prepared to sacrifice their vocation for the revolution.

He said,

> The revolution must understand that reality, and consequently must act in such a way that the entire sector of artists and intellectuals who are not genuinely revolutionary find a place to work and to create within the Revolution, so that their creative spirit will have an opportunity and freedom for expression within the revolution, even though they are not revolutionary writers or artists. That means that within the Revolution, everything goes; against the Revolution nothing ... What are the rights of the revolutionary and non-revolutionary writers and artists? Within the Revolution everything, against the Revolution, no rights at all. (Castro 1961)

Castro's presentation strikes me in two contrasting ways. It provides a litmus test of what norms and policies will continue to defend the uniqueness and populist credentials of Cuban socialism. It is this historic *Fidelista* commitment to the principles of socialist revolution that continues to give one hope that Cuba will continue to opt for a socialist outcome. On the other hand, this pronouncement is closely aligned with the Castro leadership and insufficiently a collectivist, societal project that aims for a participatory socialist democracy from below.

However, in both these approaches, worker cooperatives can play a major role in Cuban developments, rather than the country maintaining its state socialist traditions or taking a path to a quick fix by re-establishing forms of liberal or even neoliberal capitalism (Rattner 2016).

I am confident that Cuban cooperatives, as opposed to private entrepreneurial initiatives, are unlikely to be reversed in any future Cuban scenario. They will act as institutions based on worker autonomy and collective and democratic decision-making most likely immune from a Cuban capitalist insurgency if and when the US embargo is finally lifted. Cooperatives are a worker-centered approach to the economy, and as such they create defensive structures against forms of both capitalist and state socialist economies.

Increasingly the Cuban political culture demonstrates an aversion to the bureaucratic, autocratic Communist Party leadership syndrome; nor is there a particular attraction to embracing a hierarchical neoliberal capitalist system. Rather there is a thirst for mitigating an impoverished wage system in both ideologies that undermines initiative, autonomy and democracy.

Cuba has a marvelous opportunity to establish an exemplary model for supporting and developing cooperatives in both the governmental and non-state sectors of society, led by a working class that evaluates state policies from a non-bureaucratic and non-capitalist perspective.

10 | TOWARD WORKER AUTONOMY IN THE UNITED STATES

The case for cooperatives as part of the necessary movement toward economic democracy has become more central today than ever. With neoliberal capitalism not immune from cyclical crises and existing state socialisms not offering alternatives that substantially improve the lot of the working class, cooperatives are an increasingly important social movement that accepts the market but attenuates its impact on worker autonomy. As John Restakis argues in *Humanizing the Economy: Co-operatives in the Age of Capital*, democracy and the market are not necessarily antithetical; it is when social principles are subordinated to neoliberal economic doctrines solutions are required (Restakis 2010: 19). As he writes,

> ... the absence of democracy in economics is a permanent threat to the survival of democracy in politics ... co-operativism viewed the market as an instrument equally amenable to social and communitarian control as it was to control by capital ... Co-operativism in general stayed away from a program of political control ... Nevertheless, it is this more modest, pluralist, apolitical aspect of the movement that in the end carried it farther and made it more durable than Marxism's more militant strategy. (Ibid.: 46)

As Restakis makes the case,

> ... globalization is forcing communities and nations to seek alternatives that make the market work for the many, not just the few. With the global economy in crisis and the old financial order in disarray, with the free market idea in disrepute and with the corruption bred by the absence of democratic institutions in the political and economic arenas, viable alternatives to the free market myth have never been more urgently needed than now. (Ibid.: 54)

State policies allied with mobilizing cooperative sectors from below are now called for. Eminent domain remains the key approach that aligns progressive sectors of the state and localities with the societal demand for economic justice through worker autonomy and control. In that regard, the major challenge to the proliferation of cooperatives today is the retreat of the state from its responsibility to establish societal justice and economic fairness.

The struggle today centers on a revival of working-class activism combined with the recuperation of the state's responsibility for meaningful employment and the general welfare of all its citizens. In the United States we are surrounded by growing poverty and unemployment, increasing amounts of unprotected informal labor and stagnant wage levels, exacerbating the gap between the rich minority asset holders and the rest of society. The regressive data in the United States are formidable. The wages of the bottom 90 percent have been stagnant since the mid-1970s even as worker productivity has surged (Gutting and Anderson 2015). Average earnings for the top 10 percent grew more than 9 percent from 2010 to 2013 while those of the remaining income groups stagnated or shrank. Between 2007 and 2013 the earnings of the middle fifth (read middle-class workers) fell from $53,000 to $47,000 (Reuters 2015b).

Assets and stock profits continue to rise disproportionately to wages and salaries and economic growth itself (Piketty 2014). Income for the top 1 percent rose by 31 percent from 2009 to 2012 while that of the bottom 40 percent fell by 6 percent (Lowrey 2013). The Gini index of inequality in the US worsened to Third World levels; the European Union countries being in the upper .2 range while the US is at .47 (perfect income distribution being 0 and skewed income distribution being .5). This is best represented by the wealthy in America receiving less than 9 percent of their wealth via salaries and 73 percent from capital gains and interest income (Stiglitz 2012). And as is well known, the 1 percent wealthiest minority save more of their income than the 99 percent who are much more likely to spend their earnings on goods and services, thus stimulating the overall economy. The growing economic malaise in the United States is exemplified by the increasing number of workers that are underemployed and looking for full-time jobs, combined with those who are unemployed. These combined figures have now reached 13.8 percent. Much of the hiring that occurs has been concentrated in the low-wage service sectors such as retailing, home healthcare and food preparation, and in other contingent jobs. These are particularly in job areas that cannot be outsourced and where the creation of community-based cooperatives could well make an important contribution to economic growth and well-being. As opposed to corporate equity firms with their bottom-line profit orientation, cooperatives would be more likely to hire full-time employees rather than part-time contingent workers who can easily be fired.

The power exerted by the wealthy sectors impacts a society's economic growth as well as societal equity and justice for middle- and working-class sectors. Thus cooperative development faces the benign neglect, if not clear opposition, of the 1 percent, and it becomes necessary for the state to combine with working-class interests for the good not only of economic growth but of societal equity. But even without positive governmental intervention on behalf of cooperatives, cooperatives still demonstrate the capacity and willingness of the 99 percent to control and manage society at large (Marcuse 2015). However, the greatest challenge within capitalist-state arrangements is the myths and fallacies surrounding the role of government, its capacity to engineer change and its potential for public policy interventions along with its traditional fiscal and monetary roles. The role of government leadership, whether local or national, is crucial in supplying the legal, economic and moral support to produce authentic and viable cooperative development.

In the US context, we do have the interesting example of state ownership of the Bank of North Dakota (BND), which uniquely focuses on North Dakota economic development and employment stimulus. Deposits are not accepted from out-of-state businesses; a business has to have a physical North Dakota address. The BND does not compete with equity capital banks' use of ATM cards, debit and credit cards, nor online bill-paying. Only standard checking and savings accounts are available for North Dakota residents. They are a major provider of credit and loans to cooperatives and create or preserve 150,000 rural-based jobs annually. BND is a sterling example of a bank that consolidates college student loans with low interest rates and no additional fees. Students transfer their loans with interest rates as high as 14 percent to BND and achieve new variable interest rates of 2 percent and fixed rates of 5 percent.

The case study of the small Nanjie village in Henan Province in China bears examination as an example of how a group of six cooperatives based on collective ownership, production and distribution while minimizing market economics can survive and flourish. The experiment demonstrates that it makes all the difference when administrative and economic power is in the hands of local and regional governments (Ratner 2015). These are features embedded in the growth and development of the cooperative sector of the social economy. There is little question that there has to be a significant shift in the balance among state, civil society and capital in favor of the former two. The Emilia Romagna success story bears this out, as these Italian cooperatives have thrived as alternatives to monopoly capital (Restakis 2010: 55–7). As in Argentina, cooperatives in Emilia Romagna exist in all sectors of the economy, from agriculture and services to industrial production, and, as in Argentina, they have understood the value of community outreach and support as well as the need to develop networks of linked cooperatives. The multiplication of cooperatives in the Emilia Romagna industrial belt depended upon the alliance of left-wing regional governments from the mid-1970s and the tapping of the ingenuity of working-class cooperative artisan culture (ibid.: 79–85). As with the Mondragón case, depicted below, the Italian Emilia Romagna model demonstrates its resistance to equity multinational firms without a homeland and without ties to their communities.

When the United Steelworkers (USW) signed an agreement with representatives of the Mondragón cooperative in 2009 to develop a Union-Cooperative Model, this connection symbolized that US labor unions, at least those with some innovative thinking, realized that the traditional collective bargaining and continuing worker givebacks had reached their nadir and that another approach might stem the seemingly irreversible decline of worker rights in the US. The USW and Mondragón chose wisely since the Spanish/Basque Mondragón was the world's largest and most successful industrial, service and financial cooperative and USW was the largest US industrial labor union with 1.2 million members.

To combine a cooperative work organization with a union orientation will exact some compromises from each model of behavior but may result in a liaison that responds to a corporate model that is particularly ruthless within US capitalism. Normally unions have shied away from collaboration with cooperatives since their view of cooperatives is often that they are simply small-scale employers like any other enterprise and are lost to the trade union movement. Even in countries with a plethora of cooperatives, labor unions are not able to abandon their traditional approach to collective bargaining between subordinated labor unions and capital priorities. Cooperative leaders and members see most unions as lacking an understanding of the potential capacity of workers to establish autonomous enterprises without the imposition of capitalist domination. Nor do unions seem to accept that cooperatives have the capacity to more easily achieve a working-class identity than labor unions negotiating with capital over wages.

What can we learn from the most conspicuously successful multinational cooperative, which has captured some US union leaderships' admiration? The Mondragón cooperative story is by now well known (Wright 2010: 240–6). It is estimated to have over 80,000 worker-owners in 110 cooperatives, including 147 subsidiaries and 14,000 workers outside of Spain, with assets of 36 billion euros and revenues of 14 billion euros. It incorporates a university that teaches 10,000 students each year; it includes 2,000 researchers at fifteen research centers, 3,000 students enrolled in Cooperative Training Centers and 400 in Leadership and Team Work Programs (Alperovitz and Hanna, in Davis et al. 2014: 9).

The impact of the iconic cooperative, founded almost sixty years ago by the Spanish priest José María Arizmendiarrieta, carries great hopes and aspirations as its regional, national and global development proceeds. Its major approach to democratically oriented business development has been a key factor in its success. As David Ellerman notes,

> In a democratic company (e.g. an industrial cooperative) where power comes from below, then management has less of a leg to stand on to opposed new enterprise creation through spin-offs and breakaways. That has certainly been the experience of today's best example of cooperative development, the Mondragón group of cooperatives in the Basque region of Spain. The Mondragón companies produce a rather full variety of high value-added consumer products, intermediate goods, and capital goods including the first robots and computer numerically

controlled machinery designed and built in Spain. Since the firms are all cooperatives, it was all done with no foreign ownership. The group started with a single company in the mid-1950s producing a kerosene heater. Then it systematically implemented the economic principle of plentitude by filling out the backward linkages through import replacement, producing the machines to make the heaters and then the machines to make those machines. Through multiproduct diversification (new products using existing technologies), it started producing other consumer durables (stoves, refrigerators, and washing machines) and all the things to produce those things. Each bottleneck called forth new energies to solve problems, for example, a bank to help finance new enterprises, an applied technological research institute to systematically learn new technologies and turn them into new products, a consulting company to help catalyze the process of spinoffs, an insurance company for members, and a polytechnic university …

Far from a fetter on entrepreneurship, a cooperative structure is the natural setting to economically implement the principle of plenitude of growth through offspring. Here again, we see the Mondragón complex as illustrating this possibility by developing second-tier cooperatives to foster and catalyze the entrepreneurial process of growth through spin-offs in niche-filling small and medium-sized firms. (Ellerman 2013: 350–51, 353)

Complementing this analysis, Amanda Latinne, in *The Mondragón Cooperatives: Workplace Democracy and Globalization*, traces the complicated evolution of Mondragón with a dispassionate and critical eye (Latinne 2014). She brings an understanding of the complicated world of a cooperative turned corporate entity, where its economic survival and growth confront corporate ideology and culture.

Arizmendiarrieta, as a progressive Spanish priest, was cognizant not only of the liberal papal encyclical *Rerum Novarum* of 1891 but of the writings of Robert Owen, detailing his experiences in creating self-contained cooperatives in nineteenth-century England (see Chapter 1). Very early in the cooperative's development, a cooperative bank, Caja Laboral Popular, was set up which allowed for independent financing that was crucial in the early years of Mondragón's trajectory (Schweickart 2011: 67), as well as the establishment of their own social security and pension system, since the workers were considered self-employed under Spanish law (Latinne 2014: 20). Very early in Mondragón's development, it was decided that worker-owners could not sell their shares individually; it had to be a majority decision within the General Assembly of the worker-owners (ibid.: 26). This was all in the context of a regional Republican Basque progressive nationalism and culture focused on grassroots democracy, which provided Mondragón with major political and legislative support.

What also aided Mondragón was that in the Francisco Franco and post-Franco years, the Spanish governments provided significant cooperative legal and tax concessions. Moreover, in the 1950s and 1960s the Spanish government's import substitution industrialization policies allowed for significant tariff protection for domestic economic development. And, again, in the post-Franco period, the Spanish Constitution of 1978 favored the promotion of the social economy and cooperative partnerships, and the Basque region achieved degrees of autonomy in which its government pledged to support the cooperative movement (ibid.: 61,100). Thus, significant for this book's thesis, Mondragón had both significant internal cooperative values and external public policy support and public entity confederates and allies.

Latinne shows how over time Mondragón moved from an organizational direct democracy to a representative democracy, and the influence gap between cooperative manager-owners and worker-owners grew (ibid.: 36, 51; see also Whyte and Whyte 1988). Nevertheless, the Mondragón 6:1 and 9:1 ratios of skilled and highly skilled technical managers' to workers' compensation is far from the gaps we see in traditional capitalist enterprises, where typical corporate managers can be paid up to 400 times the wages paid to the company workforce.

More significant was the development of Mondragón's employment policy, which saw the number of its temporary workers (*trabajadores por cuenta ajena*) and provisional employees (*eventuales*) rise to 30 percent, receiving 80 percent of the wages of the worker-owners and contracts for up to three years, unusual in itself (Latinne 2014: 104, 114). By 2008 about half its international workforce were not worker-owners. This phenomenon ran parallel with the delocalization to China, India, Thailand, Brazil and Mexico and to eastern European countries such as Poland. While Mondragón in Spain produced high-tech, high-value-added industrial goods such as buses, kitchen appliances and machine tools, their simpler derivatives were made abroad. In this sense a certain home-country rent dividend to its worker-owners resulted from this relationship.

Despite these overseas investments, the worldwide economic crisis between 2008 and 2010 resulted in the bankruptcy of Fagor, one of Mondragón's key industrial cooperatives, the producer of major kitchen appliances. The claim was that in order for Fagor to stay competitive it had in 2005 bought out a French company, Elco-Brandt, and overreached. Others argue that Fagor was forced to expand or risk being absorbed by another foreign company, thereby losing its cooperative structure (ibid.: 97). Spain's entry into the European Union in 1986 caused similar economic challenges to the Mondragón cooperative working class as the NAFTA trilateral agreement caused for the US working class as its home companies looked abroad to extend their economic profit margin.

Despite these growing pains, Mondragón is still considered an exemplar of a participatory organization in which the workers have fared well (ibid.: 41). It is to Mondragón's credit that these growth problems have never been ignored and continue to be part of the cooperative corporation's ongoing internal dialogue, distinct from the economic neoliberal fundamentalism of oligarchic capitalist firms. Nor should it be forgotten that Mondragón still represents an alternative vision of using capital that essentially respects the role of its working class and tries to prevent needless wage gaps and downsizing where these are not absolutely necessary. Even then it attempts to place laid-off workers within other complementary cooperatives. As Latinne writes, 'Because even though their democratic model has been eroded, they are still aware of the difference between the individual freedoms of zapping consumers and collective freedom which can only be realized by active participation in collective power' (ibid.: 125–6).

While the collaboration between USW and Mondragón is still in development and the final outcome is yet to be weighed, it does present us with innovative thinking on the part of both entities and demonstrates the need for unionized labor to confront the decline of working-class living standards in the US. One area that would appeal to union initiatives is the cooperatives' capacity to protect their workers from the malfeasance of equity firms committed only to the unregulated pursuit of profit and the interests of their shareholders (Robb et al. 2010). In their projection of a union-cooperative model, Witherell et al. (2012) have laid out the plausible means of transplanting the Mondragón philosophy onto US labor. The major change, it is clear, would be the replacement of Mondragón's Social Council with a Union Committee, protecting the unionized cooperative worker-owner. The rest of the structure, including a board of directors and a management team, would remain the same. Given the different cultural contexts, the writers accept the possibility that if a majority of worker-owners decide not to have a Union Committee, it would be disbanded. The Union Committee's major role would be in protecting due process in disciplining workers, management–labor dispute resolutions, compensation and benefit structures and seniority rules (ibid.: 8). The assumption remains that union advocacy is needed to represent worker-owners as workers. US labor history pushes the proponents to see a contestatory relationship between the cooperative's elected managers and the rank-and-file cooperative members as inevitable.

However, having a Union Committee presents the danger of cooperative workers essentially falling back into typical business–union forms of alienation and enhancing worker rank-and-file passivity. This is especially so if the Union Committee management team is chosen from outside the cooperative worker membership. It seems a miscalculation to start union cooperatives rather than allowing cooperatives to grow and proliferate organically through the support of municipalities and state public policies. Union reflexes are hierarchical and may eventually undermine worker autonomy and solidarity. One can see this in the history of labor unions' districts and internationals imposing collective bargaining demands on striking locals (e.g. the Caterpillar strike of 2012 – see Greenhouse 2012). The union wage mentality versus cooperative profit-sharing and surplus value distribution presents us with a major ideological and cultural divide. A historical labor union reflex can deprive the cooperative workers of their capacity to see themselves as not needing either hierarchical union or company masters. Abolishing the wage relationship based on command-and-produce enterprises is the goal that cooperatives are advocating. Even the most advanced and sophisticated unions focus on what they must do to keep the employer in business! With authentic cooperatives, the workers *are* the business and they focus on their own interests 100 percent of the time. A better system would be a fraternal-type arrangement where proximate affinity unions would provide start-up cooperatives with pension and medical programs bought in bulk and via leveraged buying. The largest cooperative in the US, the Cooperative Home Care Associates (CHCA), founded in 1986, joined the SEIU 1199 union in 2003 and in 2007 formed a Labor-Management Committee replacing the Worker Council (Witherell et al. 2012: 17–18). This could mean a slow loss of worker self-management to the SEIU labor bureaucrats.

In the present US setting, after the severe economic recession of 2007–09, there is the beginning of an understanding among independent progressive sectors of American society that cooperatives represent the working class in a much more fundamental fashion than labor unions during periods of sustained economic crises and downturns. That is what makes the Mondragón model so attractive to those envisioning re-establishing working-class powers through the proliferation of worker cooperatives in the US and has now piqued the interest of the largest industrial union in the US, the United Steel Workers (USW).

A question that continues to be raised about Mondragón is how it can, as an international competitive corporation, maintain its commitment to democratic self-management and inter-cooperative solidarity (Azevedo and Gitahy 2010: 17). For, example in 2008, Mondragón had 129 branches, of which 75 were abroad, and of those more than half were acquisitions (ibid.: 23). As of 2014, Mondragón contained 120 cooperatives and 130 affiliates and subsidiaries with 85,000 member-owners and 15,000 employees, and achieved 30 billion euros in sales. Nevertheless, 45 percent of its profits were distributed to its workers, an additional 45 percent was reinvested and only 10 percent was channeled into administrative costs (Freundlich 2014). Crucial to the appeal of Mondragón is the cooperative's position that it serves as a basic school for worker self-management, the largest investment of time in a worker's life (Davidson 2011). Second, Mondragón's use of capital is not simply aimed at accumulating profit but rather reinvesting in workers' self-development and education on the job (Schwartz 2009; Schweickart 2011). Mondragón's cooperative bank, the Caja Laboral, has been ranked among the top 100 most efficient financial institutions in the world in terms of profit/asset ratio (Schweickart 2011: 68).

In 2009 Mondragón was selected as one of the ten most admired knowledge enterprises in Europe, based on such facets as developing knowledge-based products and solutions, maximizing enterprise intellectual capital, creating an environment for collaborative knowledge sharing, creating a learning organization and transforming corporate knowledge into stakeholder values. Mondragón shared the award with such corporations as the British Broadcasting Company and British Petroleum from the United Kingdom, Ericsson and Ikea from Sweden, Nokia from Finland, Royal Dutch Shell from the Netherlands/United Kingdom and SAP and Siemens from Germany (Teleos report, 1 December 2009).

Mondragón and its worker self-management cooperatives have been particularly embedded in their communities, making societal connections that reinforce their ideology and foster public support for further cooperative developments (Azevedo and Gitahy 2010: 6–7). Under economic crisis conditions, Mondragón attempts in the first instance to train and transfer workers from the afflicted cooperative to those on a sound footing and/or to embark on the workers' education and re-education to make job insertion and future transfers possible (ibid.: 13–14, 21).

In the US setting, United Steel Workers (USW) and Mondragón have collaborated in supporting a Pittsburgh green laundry that supplies sheets and pillowcases to universities, hospitals and hotels. The USW has supported the creation of the Cincinnati Union Cooperative Initiative, which is supporting a cooperative that retrofits buildings for energy efficiency, and an Our Harvest cooperative, again anchored in institutions like hospitals, universities and hotels, which buy produce that is grown, harvested and packaged by cooperative worker-owners (Dean 2013). These kinds of interlocking commercial connections are important to the success of cooperatives and require a type of municipal oversight that is critical as a model of future cooperative proliferation in the US.

In Cleveland, there are several interconnected cooperatives functioning as Evergreen Energy Solutions manufacturing solar panels, Evergreen Cooperative Laundry and Green City Growers Cooperative focusing on urban organic farming (Clay 2013). Begun as a coming together of public subsidies, foundation support and private capital, the Cleveland project is a successful model in that large, non-profit anchor institutions, such as hospitals (e.g. Cleveland Clinic), universities (e.g. Case Western Reserve) and museums (e.g. Cleveland Museum of Art) receive millions of dollars in local, state and federal government funds that create an environment to sustain this network of community-based worker cooperatives (Thomas Hanna, in Davis et al. 2014: 20). Very crucially, and following the Mondragón model, 10 percent of pre-tax profits are plowed back into the cooperatives' fund for the development of new jobs through additional cooperatives. Thus the focus is on asset proliferation that provides long-term stability and growth for the community. It is important to remember that one of the very first goals of the founder of Mondragón, Father Arizmendiarreta, was to develop local industry and job opportunities for this Basque region of Spain, so that the young people there would not leave for major urban hubs in search of employment, maintaining the viability of the Mondragón community. Again, taking a page out of the Mondragón experience, the Cleveland cooperatives have created Evergreen Business Services, which provides management expertise should cooperatives need technical support (Alperovitz et al. 2010).

John Clay writes of the sustainability of cooperatives in the Canadian context. For example, in a 2008 study by Quebec's Ministry of Economic Development it found that cooperatives' ten-year survival rate was 44 percent compared to 20 percent for private businesses; the Canadian Center for Community Renewal found five-year survival rates in British Columbia to be 66 percent for cooperatives and 38 percent for conventional businesses (Clay 2013). This conforms to the data we have within the Argentine context (depicted in earlier chapters). Overall, the Cleveland model has a decidedly positive impact on confronting urban decay, creating jobs, stemming poverty and creating an asset base for future cooperative urban development. Other US cities, such as Richmond, CA, Atlanta and Washington, DC, are investigating the Cleveland cooperative experience.

The economic global crisis of 2007 and beyond, with its origins in the US hyper-financialization syndrome, has given rise to an ever greater need for community-based worker-owned and -managed cooperatives. According to one report, a growing consensus is developing among many sectors of social activists and academics of varying ideological positions acknowledging the need to rethink and regenerate more community-based forms of economic development, leading to a stakeholder society as opposed to a shareholder society; that is to say toward a solidarity economy. James Gustave Speth writes that over time a shift in the multiple ownership of wealth toward a cooperative framework would lead to greater economic equality (Alperovitz et al. 2015: 15).

This is certainly borne out by Mondragón's nurturing of their community relationships and special place within the Basque region of Spain, as they have progressed to become a major cooperative corporation. Complementing this approach to development, we find another valuable model of cooperative behavior in European financial cooperative banks (such as Mondragón's Caja Laboral), which outperformed investor-owned banks before, during and after the global financial crisis of 2007–10 (Birchall 2013; also see Guardian Reports 2013). In the structure and ideology of the almost 4,000 European cooperative banks, with 50 million members and assets of almost 6 billion euros, there is much to be gleaned concerning the potential role of worker cooperatives challenging the profit-driven motives of equity flight capital (Birchall 2013: 13).

By and large, cooperative banks, particularly in Europe, have grown, kept credit flowing to small and medium-sized enterprises and remained stable while maintaining employment in their communities by focusing on customer-member ownership needs that provides them with an outlook very distinct from that of traditional capitalist banks. The focus, as in all cooperatives, is on long-term relationships with customers rather than on making profits for shareholders. These cooperative banks came through the financial crisis of 2008 and beyond without ceasing to lend to individuals and businesses, in contrast to the bailouts required within 'casino capitalism' (ibid.: 2). The cooperative banks suffered much less than investor-owned banks because they did not take part in risky and speculative ventures that caused the depression. They were also not subjected to hot foreign capital later withdrawn in the economic downturn. They remain close to their local economies and maintain efficient, low-cost banking centered on close relationships with consumer-owners, producing local ties and networks (ibid.: 34–5).

Cooperative banks pursue a different objective in that they maximize consumer surplus rather than maximizing profits. They focus mainly on recycling savings into loans and are not dependent on money markets and speculative investments. At the same time their egalitarian management profile and culture work against excessive management remuneration. Thus they maintain a low level of assets yet high rates of return and maintain economic solvency compared to investor-owned traditional banks (Birchall 2013: 20). The reason for this, comparable to worker cooperatives' approach, is that they focus on reinvestment and long-term outlooks rather than quarterly distribution of profits to shareholders. The cooperative banks were dramatically less exposed to toxic and subprime mortgages and building booms and thus came through the economic crisis better than traditional investor banks. Between 2003 and 2010 European cooperative banks enjoyed a return of 7.5 percent while investor-owned banks had returns of 5.7 percent (ibid.: 24).

Since the cooperative banks' owners and customers are one and the same there is little conflict of interest. On the other hand, we know from the US context that equity bank shareholders have limited liability as they look for high-risk gains since they are not necessarily the banks' customers. Cooperative banks, because they do not have to pay external shareholders, can reduce the margin between the interest they charge to borrowers and pay to savers. Consequently, they attract more deposits and develop comfortable liquidity with high deposit-to-loan ratios and remain immune from the demands of immediate returns characteristic of the short-term horizons of investor-owned banks (ibid.: 36). In contrast to 'too big to fail' investor banks, cooperative banks have been able to smooth out gains and losses during the peaks and troughs of the business cycle (ibid.: 37).

Comparable to the worker cooperatives we have studied, cooperative banks, because of the influence of their worker-owners, are more likely to make loans to lower-income groups with little collateral and avoid lending to companies that customers regard as unethical (ibid.: 39). Reflecting Mondragón's structural stance, most cooperative banks set up networks or federations that increase their economies of scale in education, production development, marketing and training, giving them a wider connection to their community. Also, like Mondragón, they invest in insurance, asset management and information technology. Like worker cooperatives, financial cooperatives foster local development and reinvest in local ventures and businesses, keeping a community stable and keeping people from emigrating; they invest in people that other commercial banks would not touch, thus increasing the communities' tax base (ibid.: 42–3). As Birchall reminds us, 'like other types of cooperatives, they are people-centered businesses, owned by the people they serve! This makes them more challenging ... to promote, but also much more sustainable' (ibid.: 53).

On-the-ground evidence among cooperative workers makes clear that the unique organization and economic democracy practiced in their daily routines becomes a foundation for their autonomy as workers. In a book edited by Cornwell et al. (2014) there is much documentation that confirms cooperatives as unique work environments. Within the Connecticut River Valley, cooperative workers report that they need not hide their opinions and feelings for fear of losing their jobs and are able to cultivate their 'true selves.' For this reason they would prefer their job to making more pay elsewhere because they can live according to their closest-held values (ibid.: 23). Workers put these values into practice in democratic decision-making every day, not just once every two years at the voting booths (ibid.: 32). Arbitrary decisions from bosses or managers from above are absent and in their place are lateral decisions among their equals. 'With the support of their co-workers, members can leave in the middle of the day for a personal or family emergency, to get a check cashed, pick up the kids or meet the plumber if those needs come up.' This flexibility empowers workers to be more involved with aspects of their lives outside of work, such as their families, communities, hobbies and civic organizations (ibid.: 25). This is markedly different from the typical US hierarchical firm in which only 12 percent of workers have access to paid family leave (Cain Miller and Streitfeld 2015).

And as is clear from Argentine cooperatives as well, if there is a loss of business, the workers absorb the loss collectively and, by the same token, benefit from an improvement in conditions. As one cooperative worker said, 'We almost always had debates about how much we could afford to pay over market and how much more was going to our mission but all those years ... we never once had a debate about increasing the amount of money that came to our-selves' (Cornwell et al. 2013: 33). Most cooperatives work by con-sensus decision-making which can be painfully slow to achieve but once achieved breeds much stronger worker solidarity than decisions based on majority rule, which may leave the minority at loggerheads. There is then less resentment at the decisions taken and more traction moving forward (ibid.: 52–4). As Restakis depicts the difference between the cooperative and capitalist firms, 'In one, the enterprise is a means to human fulfillment of all through the creation of community. In the other, the enterprise is a means for the fulfillment of some through the subordination of others' (Restakis 2010: 239).

In conclusion

This book has dealt with the major challenges to the development of cooperatives as autonomous working-class enterprises in response to the retreat of the state in capitalist countries and the state socialist bureaucracy's adapting to cooperative worker ownership and management in the Cuban case. In both the capitalist and socialist contexts, cooperatives represent a creative response to unemployment and poverty within these contemporary economies. Cooperatives represent an adventurous re-envisioning of work organization, democratic procedures, the reality of employee self-management and autonomy, and the fostering of community and political outreach. These combined features provide an alternative to the hierarchical private firm's role and the socialist state-centered primordial monopoly in the economy and society.

The potential uses of eminent domain to meet this challenge in the United States represent and incorporate public policies that provide laborers and employees with the legitimacy to own and run their own enterprises. Eminent domain, the constitutional process, has a basis in public policy, which includes the powers to tax and spend, to zone for economic purposes, to impose environmental regulations, and to avoid neighborhood blight. Worker control requires the implementation of eminent domain on behalf of laborers and employees for the clear benefits of economic development and social and economic justice, as well as worker autonomy. As cooperatives represent labor and as they accumulate capital, they can clearly eliminate the need for capitalists. In the Cuban case, cooperative developments in agriculture, services and industry provide the system with a democratization of the economy, allowing the working class to achieve a sense of autonomy and control in the workplace. In both the neoliberal capitalist system and the state socialist system, the state apparatus continues to represent capital, in the hands of the large hierarchical firms or state capital managers. In both cases the opportunities for the development of grassroots economic democracy are blocked and working-class autonomy is thwarted. Worker cooperative movements require public policy renovation that is based on local and community interactions within the working class itself. The very democratic instinct of worker cooperatives represents their greatest strength as well as their greatest challenge to business as usual.

As we have said, workers as subjects are more than voters and consumers, especially in the new economy dominated by neoliberal capitalism. In this new form of post-capitalist society workers have the potential, in ways that Marx would uphold, to provide a strong counterpoint to capitalism run amok. They represent human capital without which capitalism cannot survive in its current form and which provides them with the leverage to challenge it from within. They are a workforce that is potentially far more than workers producing a product. They can reappropriate their lives beyond their existence in production. They are cultural beings, not simply cogs in a machine or a service provider. Cooperatives and recuperated enterprises bring the whole life of the worker beyond his/her simple place as a worker for someone else into play. As Marx indicated, labor is capital and capital is labor. Cooperatives make this clearer than any other institution by clarifying the exploitative nature of the pre-cooperative worker engagement, while at the same time enhancing their human values. To be whole, workers require rest, recreation, conversation and, above all, decision-making power rather than simply keeping their noses to the grindstone. Cooperatives are basic to human development because their success depends on the emancipation of the whole worker rather than what the erstwhile capitalist wanted of them and determined for them. Pursuing human development beyond immediate production values through worker cooperatives is a process now under way that will continue to challenge neoliberal capitalism and state socialism.

REFERENCES

Abell, H. (2014) *Worker Cooperatives: Pathways to Scale*, Takoma Park, MD: The Democracy Collaborative.

Abidor, M. (2015) *Voices of the Paris Commune*, Oakland, CA: PM Press.

Aiziczon, F. (2007) 'El Clasismo revisitado. La impronta del trotskismo en la politización del sindicato ceramista,' Mimeo, Zanón Bajo Control Obrero.

— (2015) 'La experiencia ceramista: clasismo y autogestión obrera,' Paper presented at workshop on Empresas Recuperadas, Instituto de Investigaciones Gino Germani, University of Buenos Aires, 27–29 October.

Alperovitz, G. (2013) Conference on Universities for the New Economy, New School University, 13 April, and in J. Shantz and J. Brendan Macdonald, *Beyond Capitalism*, New York: Bloomsbury.

Alperovitz, G., T. Williamson and T. Howard (2010) 'The Cleveland model,' *The Nation*, 1 March.

Alperovitz, G., J. G. Speth and J. Guinan (2015) 'The next system project: new political-economic possibilities for the 21st century,' March, thenextsystem.org/wp-content/uploads/2015/03/NSPReport1_Digital.pdf.

Amin, S. (2013) *The Implosion of Contemporary Capitalism*, New York: Monthly Review Press.

Area Estudios y Estadística: Informe 4to. Trimestre, INDEC, 2015.

Azevedo, A. and L. Gitahy (2010) 'The cooperative movement, self-management and competitiveness: the case of the Mondragón Corporación Cooperativa,' *Working USA: The Journal of Labor and Society*, 13(1): 5–29.

Azzellini, D. (2013) 'From cooperatives to enterprises of direct social property in the Venezuelan process,' in C. Piñeiro Harnecker (ed.), *Cooperatives and Socialism: A View from Cuba*, London and New York: Palgrave Macmillan.

Barrera Rodríguez, S. (2015) 'Empresas mixta estado-cooperativa: una propuesta,' 30 October, www.perfiles.cult.cu/article.php?article_id=291#sdendnote2sym.

Bayer, O. (2015) 'En defense del trabajo,' *Página 12*, 23 December.

Beerman, J. M. and J. W. Singer (1989) 'Baseline questions in legal reasoning: the example of property in jobs,' *Georgia Law Review*, 23: 911–95.

Benkler, Y. (2015) 'Peer mutualism and the future of capitalism,' Paper presented at New School Conference on Digital Labor, 13–14 November.

Bernanke, B. S. (2006) 'Global economic integration: what's new and what's not?,' Remarks at the Federal Reserve Bank of Kansas City's Thirtieth Annual Economic Symposium, 25 August.

Bernstein, E. (1993) *The Preconditions of Socialism*, London: Cambridge University Press.

Birchall, J. (2013) *Resilience in a Downturn: The Power of Financial Cooperatives*, Geneva: International Labor Organization, 20 March.

Blackstone, W. (2014 [1766]) *Commentaries on the Laws of England: The Rights of Persons*, First Rate Publishers, online.

Block, F. L. (1996) *The Vampire State*, New York: New Press.

Bluestone, B. and B. Harrison (1982) *Deindustrialization of America: Plant Closings, Community Abandonment and the Dismantling of Basic Industry*, New York: Basic Books.

Bottomore, T. B. (1961) *Marx's Concept of Man* (with an Afterword by Erich Fromm), New York: Frederick Ungar Publishing Co.

Braverman, H. (1974) *Labor and Monopoly Capital*, New York: Monthly Review Press.

Bray, J. F. (1839) *Labor's Wrongs and Labor's Remedies*, Whitefish, MT: Kessinger Legacy Reprints.

Briner, M. A. and A. Cusmano (2003) 'Las empresas recuperadas en la Ciudad de Buenos Aires: una aproximación a partir del estudio de siete experiencias,' in *Empresas Recuperadas: Ciudad de Buenos Aires*, Buenos Aires: Secretaría de Desarrollo Económico, Gobierno de la Ciudad de Buenos Aires.

Burgerman, S. D. (1998) 'Mobilizing principles: the role of transnational activists in promoting human rights principles,' *Human Rights Quarterly*, 20(4): 905–23.

Buttigieg, A. J. (2005) 'The contemporary discourse on civil society,' *Boundary*, 2: 33–52.

Cafardo, A. and P. Domínguez Font (2003) *Autogestión obrera en el siglo XXI*, Cuaderno de Trabajo no. 27, Buenos Aires: Centro Cultural de la Cooperación.

Cain Miller, C. and D. Streitfeld (2015) 'Leaps in leave, if only parents would take it,' *New York Times*, 2 September.

Campos Santos, P. (2012a) 'El enemigo, el contrario y las leyes de la dialéctica,' *Boletín SPD* (Socialismo Participativo y Democratico), 124: 1–3.

— (2012b) 'Sobre la elección del presidente y vicepresidente por medio del sufragio universal,' *Boletín SPD*, 120, 18 September.

— (2015) 'Cumple siete años el Movimiento por un Socialismo Particpativo y Democrático,' *Havana Times*, 17 August.

— (2016a) 'El gran error de la izquierda: confundir estatalismo con socialismo,' *Boletín SPD*, 189, 1 February.

— (2016b) 'Grave error topar los precios: siete medidas para ayudar a solucionar el problema,' *Observatorio Crítico Cubano*, 17 January.

Carpenter, Z. (2015) 'The staggering lopsided economic recovery,' *The Nation*, 26 January.

Carroll, W. K. (2010) *The Making of a Transnational Capitalist Class*, London: Zed Books.

Castro, F. (1961) 'Palabras a los intelectuales,' Havana: National Cultural Council, 30 June.

Chaguaceda, A. (2015) 'The promise besieged: participation and autonomy in Cuba,' in P. Brenner et al. (eds), *The Revolution under Raúl Castro: A Contemporary Cuban Reader*. Lanham, MD: Rowman and Littlefield, pp. 111–16.

Chatterjee, P. (2004) *The Politics of the Governed*, New York: Columbia University Press.

Chomsky, N. (2013) 'What is the common good?,' *Journal of Philosophy*, CX(12): 685–700.

Clark, A. M., E. Friedman and K. Hochstetter (1998) 'The sovereign limits of global civil society,' *World Politics*, 51(1): 1–35.

Clay, J. (2013) 'Democratic promise,' *Truthout*, 14 July.

Cornwell, J., M. Johnson and A. Trott (2014) *Building Co-operative*

Power: Stories and Strategies from Worker-Cooperatives in the Connecticut River Valley, Amherst, MA: Levellers Press.

Dahl, R. A. (1985) *A Preface to Economic Democracy*, Berkeley: University of California Press.

Davidson, C. (2011) *New Paths to Socialism: Essays on the Mondragon Cooperatives and Workplace Democracy, Green Manufacturing Structural Reform, and the Politics of Transition*, Pittsburgh, PA: Changemaker Publications.

Davis, J., T. Hanna, L. Krimerman and A. Mcleod (2014) 'Scaling up the cooperative movement. A project of grassroots economic organizing with the democratic collaborative,' community-wealth.org/sites/clone. community-wealth.org/files/ downloads/book-davis-hanna-krimerman-mcleod.pdf.

Davis, P. and M. Parker (2007) 'Cooperatives, labor, and the state: the English economists revisited,' *Review of Radical Political Economics*, 39(4): 523–42.

Dean, A. B. (2013) 'Why unions are going into the co-op business,' *Yes!* magazine, 5 March.

Dewan, S. (2013) 'A city invokes seizure laws to save homes,' *New York Times*, 29 July.

Di Marco, G., H. Palomino et al. (2003) *Movimientos sociales en la Argentina*, Buenos Aires: Jorge Baudino Ediciones.

Diaz, B. (2012) *Cooperatives within Cuba's Current Economic Model*, Havana: Flacso.

— (2013) Presentation at seminar on 'Socialist Renovation and Capitalist Crisis,' University of Havana, 26 June.

Díaz, C. (2015) 'Sobre el accionar de la izquierda demócratica y socialista,' *Boletín SPD*, 166, July.

Díaz Fernandez, I. (2015) 'El sector no-estatal de la economía cubana,' Presentation at Columbia University Institute of Latin American Studies, 16 November.

Djilas, M. (1957) *The New Class*, New York: Praeger.

Durgan, A. (2011) 'Workers' democracy in the Spanish Revolution, 1936–1937,' in I. Ness and D. Azzellini (eds), *Ours to Master and to Own: Workers' Control from the Commune to the Present*, Chicago, IL: Haymarket Books.

ECLAC (2012) *Structural Change for Equality: An Integrated Approach to Development*, Santiago: United Nations.

Edwards, M. (2004) *Civil Society*, Cambridge: Polity Press.

Ellerman, D. (1984) 'Workers' cooperatives: the question of legal structure,' in R. Jackall and H. M. Levin (eds), *Worker Cooperatives in America*, Berkeley: University of California Press.

— (2013) 'Three themes about democratic enterprises: capital structure, education and spin-offs,' in D. Kruse (ed.), *Sharing Ownership, Profits and Decision-Making in the 21st Century Advances in the Economic Analysis of Participatory and Labor-Managed Firms*, London: Emerald Group Publishing.

— (2015) 'On the renting of persons: the neo-abolionist case against today's peculiar institution,' *Economic Thought*, 4(1): 1–20.

Erdal, D. (2011) *Beyond the Corporation: Humanity Working*, London: Bodley Head.

Fajn, G. (2003) *Fábricas y empresas recuperadas*, Buenos Aires: Centro Cultural de la Cooperación.

Fernández, O. (2015) 'Las territorias cubanos ante las reformas institutionales del último lustro,' Presentation at CUNY Bildner Center conference on 'Update on Cuban Economy and US–Cuban Relations,' 1 June.

Fernández Aballí, C. (2015) Presentation at CUNY Bildner Center conference on 'US–Cuba: Normalization and Reforms,' 28 August.

Feuer, A. (2016) 'Uber drivers up against the app,' *New York Times*, 21 February.

Fields, Z. (2008) 'Efficiency and equity: the empresas recuperadas of Argentina,' *Latin American Perspectives*, 35(6): 83–92.

Figueras, M. A. (2015) 'Cambios estructurales para desarrollar la economía de Cuba,' 5 May, cubaeconomía.blogspot.com/2015/05/.

Font, M. and D. Jancsics (2015) Presentation at CUNY Bildner Center on 'Spatial Differences and Disparities: Mapping and Visualization,' 1 June.

FPWA (Federation of Protestant Welfare Agencies) (2014) *Worker Cooperatives for New York City: A Vision for Addressing Income Inequality*, December.

Freundlich, F. (2014) Presentation on cooperatives at CUNY Murphy Center, 30 March.

Fromm, E. (1961) *Marx's Concept of Man*, New York: Continuum.

Fucek, H. (2011) comerciojustoargentina.blogspot.com/2011_06_01_archive.html.

Fuchs, C. (2016) 'Digital labor and imperialism,' *Monthly Review*, 67(8): 1–14.

Galbraith, J. K. (2008) *The Predator State: How Conservatives Abandoned the Free Market and Why Liberals Should Too*, New York: Free Press.

Gershon, M. and D. Lippman (2015) *New Cuban Cooperatives*, Film.

Gonzáles, L. (2015) 'La revolución cubana se extinque,' *Boletín SPD*, 166, July.

Gonzalez Corso, M. (2015) Presentation at CUNY Bildner Cener conference on 'U.S.-Cuba: Normalization and Reforms', 28 August.

Goston, L. O. (2006) 'Property rights and the common good,' *Hastings Center Report*, 36: 10–11.

Gramsci, A. (1971) *Selections from the Prison Notebooks*, New York: International Publishers.

Greenhouse, S. (2008) *The Big Squeeze: Tough Times for the American Worker*, New York: Knopf.

— (2012) 'Caterpillar workers ratify deal they dislike,' *New York Times*, 17 August.

Guanche, J. C. (2012) 'La participación ciudadana en el estado cubano,' *Temas*, 70: 69–79.

Guardian Reports (2013) 'Financial cooperatives outperform traditional banks,' *Guardian Reports*, 9 July.

Gutting, G. and E. Anderson (2015) 'What's wrong with inequality?,' *New York Times*, 23 April.

Haraszti, M. (1978) *A Worker in a Worker's State*, New York: Universe Books.

Harrington, M. P. (2002) 'Public use and the original understanding of the so-called "Takings Clause,"' *Hastings Law Journal*, 53:1245.

Harvey, D. (2012) *Rebel Cities: From the Right to the Cities to the Urban Revolution*, London: Verso.

Havana Times (2016) 'US relaxes more aspects of its embargo on Cuba,' *Havana Times*, 16 January.

Hegel, F. (1942) *Philosophy of Right*, trans. T. M. Knox, London: Oxford University Press.

Heller, P. (2004) *Fábricas Ocupadas*, Buenos Aires: Ediciones Rumbos.

Hernández, R. (2015) 'The collapse of socialism is beyond the present horizon,' in P. Brenner et al. (eds), *The Revolution under Raúl Castro: A*

Contemporary Cuba Reader, Lanham, MD: Rowman & Littlefield, pp. 83–8.

Hirschfeld Davis, J. (2015a) 'U.S. relaxes the rules on dealings with Cuba,' *New York Times*, 19 September.

— (2015b) 'U.S. commerce chief makes a pitch in Cuba,' *New York Times*, 7 October.

Hobsbawm, E. (2011) *How to Change the World: Reflections on Marx and Marxism*, New Haven, CT: Yale University Press.

Hudis, P. and K. B. Anderson (2004) *The Rosa Luxemburg Reader*, New York: Monthly Review Press.

Huws, U. (2014) *Labor in the Digital Economy*, New York: Monthly Review Press.

Itzigsohn, J. and J. Rebón (2015) 'The recuperation of enterprises: defending workers' lifeworld, creating new tools of contention,' *Latin American Research Review*, 50(4): 178–96.

Jameson, F. (2011) *Representing Capital: A Reading of Volume One*, London: Verso.

Johnson, S. and J. Kwak (2013) *White House Burning: Our National Debt and Why It Matters to You*, New York: Vintage Books.

Kamenka, E. (1983) *The Portable Marx*, New York: Penguin Books.

Keck, M. E. and K. Sikkink (1998) *Activists beyond Borders: Advocacy Networks and International Politics*, Ithaca, NY: Cornell University Press.

Kelly, M., S. Dubb, and V. Duncan (2016) *Broad-Based Ownership Models as Tools for Job Creation and Community Development*, Takoma Park, MD: The Democracy Collaborative.

Krugman, P. (2013) 'That old-time economics,' *New York Times*, 17 April.

Kulfas, M. (2003) 'El contexto económico: destrucción del aparato productivo y restructuración regresiva,' in *Empresas recuperadas: Ciudad de Buenos Aires*, Buenos Aires: Secretaría de Desarrollo Económico, Gobierno de la Ciudad de Buenos Aires.

Latinne, A. (2014) *The Mondragón Cooperatives: Workplace Democracy and Globalization*, Cambridge: Intersentia Publishing Ltd.

Lenin, V. I. (1965 [1923]) 'On cooperation,' in *Collected Works*, Moscow: Progressive Publishers.

Lepore, J. (2015) 'Richer and poorer,' *New Yorker*, 16 March.

Locke, J. (1960 [1690]) *Two Treatises of Government*, New York: New American Library.

López, A. L. and G. Buffa (2015) 'Cuba y el proceso del cooperativismo no agrario: la experiencia de la cooperativa reconstructora de vehículos CVR,' *Revista Idelcoop*, 217, November.

Lowrey, A. (2013) 'Household incomes remain flat despite improving economy,' *New York Times*, 27 September.

Lozano, C. (2005) *Los problemas de la distribución del ingreso y el crecimiento en la Argentina actual*, Buenos Aires: CTA, Instituto de Estudios y Formación.

Lukács, G. (1971 [1922]) *History and Class Consciousness*, Cambridge, MA: MIT Press.

Luxemburg, R. (1970) *Reform or Revolution*, New York: Pathfinder Press.

Lydersen, K. (2009) *Revolt on Goose Island: The Chicago Factory Takeover and What It Says about the Economic Crisis*, New York: Melville House.

— (2016) 'Chicago window workers who occupied their factory in 2008 win new bankruptcy payout,' *In These Times*, 25 January.

Lynd, S. (1981) 'What happened in Youngstown?,' *Radical America*, 15: 37–48.

Magnani, E. (2003) *El cambio silencioso: Empresas y fábricas recuperadas por los trabajadores en la Argentina*, Buenos Aires: Prometeo Libros.

Mankiw, N. G. and P. L. Swagel (2006) 'Politics and economics of offshore outsourcing,' Working paper, National Bureau of Economic Research, July.

Marcuse, P. (2015) 'Cooperatives on the path to socialism?,' *Monthly Review*, 66(9), February.

Marx, K. (1967a) *Capital*, vol. 1, New York: International Publishers.

— (1967b) *Capital*, vol. 2, New York: International Publishers.

— (1967c) *Capital*, vol. 3, New York: International Publishers.

— (1973) *Grundrisse*, New York: Vintage Books.

— (1975a) *Economic and Philosophical Manuscripts*, New York: Frederick Ungar Publishing Co.

— (1975b [1865]) *Wages, Price and Profit*, Peking: Foreign Language Press.

— (1977) *Capital*, vol. 1, New York: Vintage Books.

— (1978 [1843]) 'On the Jewish question,' in R. C. Tucker (ed.), *The Marx–Engels Reader*, New York: Norton.

— (1983 [1844]) 'From the Economic and Philosophical Manuscripts,' in E. Kamenka (ed.), *The Portable Karl Marx*, New York: Penguin.

— (1998 [1871]) *The Civil War in France*, Chicago, IL: Charles Kerr Publishing Co.

McKinley, J. (2015) 'Cuomo strikes deal to keep Alcoa plant and 600 jobs upstate,' *New York Times*, 25 November.

Medoff, P. and H. Sklar (1994) *Streets of Hope: The Fall and Rise of an Urban Neighborhood*, Boston, MA: South End Press.

Mesa-Lago, C. (2012) Presentation at CUNY Bildner Center on 'Raul Castro's Socio-Economic Reforms: Evaluation of Results,' 2 November.

Meyer, A. (2015) 'Generamos nuevos fuentes de trabajo,' *Página 12*, 11 August.

Moberg, D. (2013) 'Can manufacturing be reborn in the USA?,' *In These Times*, 22 April.

Morton, A. L. (1978) *The Life and Ideas of Robert Owen*, New York: International Publishers.

Ness, I. (2011) 'Workers' direct action and factory control in the United States,' in I. Ness and D. Azzellini (eds), *Ours to Master and to Own: Workers' Control from the Commune to the Present*, Chicago, IL: Haymarket Books, pp. 302–21.

New York Times (2015) 'The Fed's next move,' *New York Times*, 18 December.

Nova González, A. (2012) Presentation at CUNY Bildner Center on 'Forms of Property in the Cuban Economy: Agriculture,' 5 October.

— (2013) 'Sector agropecuario y lineamientos,' in M. A. Font and C. Riobó (eds), *Handbook of Contemporary Cuba: Economy, Politics, Civil Society, and Globalization*. Boulder, CO: Paradigm Publishers, pp. 81–96.

Nova González, A. and M. González-Corso (2015) Presentation at CUNY Bildner Center on 'Bilateral Trade between Cuba and US: Reality and Prospects,' 1 June.

Nzinga Ifateyo, A. (2014) 'A co-op state of mind,' *In These Times*, September.

— (2015) '$5 million for cooperative development in Madison,' Grassroots Economic Organizing (GEO).

Ocaña Díaz, O. (2016) 'El aguijón del diablo,' *Observatorio Crítico Cubano*, 26 January.

Orwell, G. (1952) *Homage to Catalonia*, New York: Harcourt, Inc.

Palomino, H. (ed.) (2010) *La Nueva Dinámica de las Relaciones Laborales en la Argentina*, Buenos Aires: Jorge Baudino Ediciones.

Pérez Villanueva, O. E. (2013) 'Updating Cuba's economic model,' in M. Font and C. Riobó (eds), *Handbook of Contemporary Cuba: Economy, Politics, Civil Society, and Globalization*, Boulder, CO: Paradigm Publishers, pp. 22–35.

— (2015a) Presentation at CUNY Bildner Center on 'Las Pequeñas y Medianas Empresas en Cuba: Utopia or Realidad,' 1 June.

— (2015b) 'Updating the Cuban economic model,' in P. Brenner et al. (eds), *The Revolution under Raúl Castro: A Contemporary Cuba Reader*, Lanham, MD: Rowman and Littlefield, pp. 139–44.

Pérez Villanueva, O. E., P. Vidal Alejandro, A. González Nova and L. Iñiguez Rojas (2012) *Miradas a la Economía Cubana*, Havana: Editorial Caminos.

Peters, P. (2015) 'Cuba's entrepreneurs,' in P. Brenner et al. (eds), *The Revolution under Raúl Castro: A Contemporary Cuba Reader*, Lanham, MD: Rowman & Littlefield, pp. 145–52.

Piketty, T. (2014) *Capital in the Twenty-First Century*, Cambridge, MA: Harvard University Press.

Piñeiro Harnecker, C. (2011) 'Empresas no estatales en la economía cubana: construyendo el socialism?,' *Temas*, 67: 68–77.

— (2012) 'Visiones sobre el socialism que guían los cambios actuales en Cuba,' *Temas*, 70: 46–55.

— (2013a) 'Cuba: realidad y perspectivas del cooperativismo,' www.centrocultural.coop/blogs/cooperativismo/2013, 28 February.

— (2013b) 'New forms of enterprise in Cuba's changing economy,' in M. A. Font and C. Riobó (eds), *Handbook of Contemporary Cuba: Economy, Politics, Civil Society, and Globalization*, Boulder, CO: Paradigm Publishers, pp. 50–63.

Pons Pérez, S. (2015a) Presentation at CUNY Bildner Center on 'Finanzas Públicas de Cuba: Posible Impacto del Nuevo Marco para las Relaciones en EEUU,' 1 June.

— (2015b) 'Tax law dilemmas for self-employed workers,' *From the Island*, 29, 20 May.

Porter, E. (2015) 'A proposal to help falls short,' *New York Times*, 15 July.

Putnam, R. D. (1993) *Making Democracy Work: Civic Traditions in Modern Italy*, Princeton, NJ: Princeton University Press.

Rameri, A. and T. Raffo (2005) *Los nuevos pobres e indigentes que arroja la inflación*, Buenos Aires: CTA Instituto de Estudios y Formación.

Rancière, J. (2013) *Dissensus: On Politics and Aesthetics*, London: Continuum.

Ranis, P. (1976) 'Descubrimiento y auto-descubrimiento,' *Arieto*, 3(2/3): 24–9.

— (1992) *Argentine Workers: Peronism and Contemporary Class Consciousness*, Pittsburgh, PA: University of Pittsburgh Press.

— (1995) *Class, Democracy and Labor in Contemporary Argentina*, New Brunswick, NJ: Transaction Publishers.

— (1999) 'The impact of state and capital policies on Argentine labor: a comparative perspective,' in J. Havet (ed.), *Identities, State and Markets*, Toronto: Canadian Scholars' Press, pp. 101–23.

— (2004) 'Rebellion, class and labor in Argentine society,' *Working USA: the Journal of Labor and Society*, 7(4): 8–35.

— (2005) 'Argentina's worker-occupied factories and enterprises,' *Socialism and Democracy*, 19 (3): 93–115.

— (2006) 'Factories without bosses: Argentina's experience with worker-run enterprises,' *Labor Studies in Working Class History of the Americas*, 3(1): 11–23.

— (2007) 'Eminent domain: unused tool for American labor,' *Working USA: the Journal of Labor and Society*, 10(2): 193–208.

— (2010) 'Argentine worker cooperatives in civil society: a challenge to capital–labor relations,' *Working USA: the Journal of Labor and Society*, 13: 77–105.

— (2011) 'Occupy Wall Street: an opening to worker-occupation of factories and enterprises in the U.S.,' *mrzine. Monthly Review*, 9 November, pp. 1–23.

— (2014) 'Promoting cooperatives by the use of eminent domain: Argentina and the United States,' *Socialism and Democracy*, 28(1): 51–69.

Ratner, C. (2015) 'Neoliberal co-optation of leading co-op organizations, and socialist counter-politics of cooperation,' *Monthly Review*, 66 (9), February.

Rattner, S. (2016) 'Capitalism will make a freer Cuba,' *New York Times*, 20 February.

Ravsberg, F. (2012) 'Unanimidad vs. institucionalidad,' *Boletin SPD*, 107, 11 July.

Rebón, J. (2004) *Desobedeciendo al desempleo: la experiencia de las empresas recuperadas*, Buenos Aires: Ediciones Picaso/La Rosa Blindada.

Restakis, J. (2010) *Humanizing the Economy: Co-operatives in the Age of Capital*, New Society Publishers.

Reuters (2015a) 'Unsatisfied by wage hike, some Walmart shareholders seek more change,' 25 February.

— (2015b) 'Middle class decline looms over final years of Obama presidency,' 18 January.

Ritter, A. R. M. (2013) 'Cuba's evolving public policies toward small enterprises,' in M. A. Font and C. Riobó (eds), *Handbook of Contemporary Cuba: Economy, Politics, Civil Society, and Globalization*, Boulder, CO: Paradigm Publishers, pp. 36–49.

— (2016) 'Alternative institutional futures for Cuba's mixed economy,' theCubaneconomy.com/articles/tag/cooperatives/, 1 February.

Robb, A. J., J. H. Smith and T. J. Webb (2010) 'Cooperative capital: what it is and why our world needs it,' Paper for EUROCSE Conference on Financial Cooperative Approaches to Local Development through Sustainable Innovation, Trento, Italy, 10/11 June.

Ruggeri, A. and M. Vieta (2015) 'Argentina's worker-recuperated enterprises, 2010–2013: a synthesis of recent empirical findings,' *Journal of Entrepreneurial and Organizational Diversity*, 4(1): 75–103.

Ruggeri, A., C. Martínez and H. Trinchero (2005) *Las empresas recuperadadas en la Argentina*, Buenos Aires: Facultad de Filosofía y Letras.

Safford, S. (2004) 'Why the Garden Club couldn't save Youngstown: civic infrastructure and mobilization in economic crises,' MIT Industrial Performance Center Working Papers, Cambridge, MA.

Schmitt, C. (2005 [1922]) *Political Ideology*, Chicago, IL: University of Chicago Press.

— (2007 [1927]) *The Concept of the Political*, Chicago, IL: University of Chicago Press.

Scholz, T. (2015) 'Unpacking platform cooperativism,' Paper presented at New School Conference on Digital Labor, 13/14 November.

Schor, J. (2015) 'How to build and sustain cooperative platforms,' Paper presented at New School Conference on Digital Labor, 13/14 November.

Schwartz, J. D. (2009) 'In Cleveland, worker co-ops look to a Spanish model,' *Time*, 22 December.

Schwartz, N. D. (2015) 'Low income workers see biggest drop in paychecks,' *New York Times*, 3 September.

— (2016) 'Economists take aim at wealth inequality,' *New York Times*, 4 January.

Schweickart, D. (2011) *After Capitalism*, Lanham, MD: Rowman & Littlefield.

Searcy, D. and R. Gebeloff (2015) 'Middle class shrinks further as more fall out instead of climbing up,' *New York Times*, 26 January.

Sitrin, M. A. (2012) *Everyday Revolutions: Horizontalism and Autonomy in Argentina*, London: Zed Books.

Skidelsky, R. (2009) *Keynes: The Return of the Master: Why, Sixty Years after His Death, John Maynard Keynes Is the Most Important Economic Thinker for America*, New York: Public Affairs Press.

Solar Cabrales, F. J. (2012) 'Las trampas en el camino,' *Boletín SPD*, 107, 11 July.

Sosa, M. (2015) Presentation at CUNY Bildner Center on 'El Desarrollo Local en Cuba: Una Arista al Desarrollo,' 1 June.

Stiglitz, J. E. (2012) *The Price of Inequality*, New York: Norton.

Sullivan, M. (2015) 'Cuba: U.S. restrictions on travel and remittances,' Congressional Research Service, 10 April.

Sundararajan, A. (2015) 'An economic perspective on cooperatives,' Paper presented at New School Conference on Digital Labor, 13/14 November.

Tarrow, S. (1998) *Power in Movement: Social Movements and Contentious Politics*, Cambridge: Cambridge University Press.

Thomas, P. D. (2010) *The Gramscian Moment: Philosophy, Hegemony and Marxism*, Chicago, IL: Haymarket Books.

Thompson, E. P. (1968) *The Making of the English Working Class*, London: Penguin.

Thompson, W. (2012 [1827]) *Labour Rewarded. The Claims of Labour and Capital Conciliated; or, How to Secure to Labour the Whole Product of Its Exertion*, Memphis, TN: General Books.

Tilly, C. (2004) *Social Movements, 1768–2004*, Boulder, CO: Paradigm Publishers.

Tirado, L. (2014) *Hand to Mouth: Living in Bootstrap America*, New York: G. P. Putnam's Sons.

Trotsky, L. (1972) *The Revolution Betrayed*, New York: Pathfinder Press.

Tucker, R. C. (ed.) (1978) *The Marx–Engels Reader*, New York: Norton.

Uchitelle, L. (2006) *The Disposable American: Layoffs and Their Consequences*, New York: Knopf.

UN (2015) *Human Development Report: Sustaining Human Progress: Reducing Vulnerabilities and Building Resilience*, New York: United Nations Development Program.

Urofsky, M. I. (2009) *Louis D. Brandeis: A Life*, New York: Pantheon.

Vales, L. (2015) 'A un paso de expropiarlo,' *Página 12*, 27 November

Vieta, M. (2009) 'The social innovations of *Autogestión* in Argentina's recuperated enterprises: cooperatively reorganizing productive life in hard times,' *Labor*.

Vuotto, M. (2015) 'Las cooperativas no agropecuarias y la transformacíon económica en Cuba: políticas, procesos y estrategías,' *Revista de Estudios Cooperativos*, 120, 14 May.

Wallis, V. (2011) 'Workers' control and revolution,' in I. Ness and D. Azzellini (eds), *Ours to Master and to Own: Workers' Control from the Commune to the Present*, Chicago, IL: Haymarket Books.

Walzer, M. (1998) 'The idea of civil society: a path to social reconstruction,' in E. J. Dionne (ed.), *Community Works: The Revival of Civil Society*, Washington, DC: Brookings Institution.

Whyte, W. Foote and K. K. Whyte (1988) *Making Mondragón: The Growth and Dynamics of the Worker Cooperative Complex*, Ithaca, NY: ILR Press.

Witherell, R., C. Cooper and M. Peck (2012) 'Sustainable jobs, sustainable communities: the Union Co-op model,' 26 March, www.usw.org/union/allies/The-Union-Co-op-Model-March-26-2012.pdf.

Wolff, R. D. (2012) *Occupy the Economy*, San Francisco, CA: City Lights Books.

Wright, E. O. (1997) *Class Counts: Comparative Studies in Class Analysis*, Cambridge: Cambridge University Press.

— (2010) *Envisioning Real Utopias*, London: Verso.

Interviews

José Abelli, 21 July, 2004
Betsy Anaya, 20 June, 2013
Eduardo Ayalla, 30 October, 2015
Walter Blanco, 20 July, 2006
Luis Caro, 13 and 19 July 2005, 24 July 2006, 8 May 2014 https://www.youtube.com/watch?V=X6Q7NpnY42Y
Cecelia Casablanca, 24 July, 2006
Martín Cossarino, 10 July, 2006
Silvia Díaz, 31 October, 2015
Hugo Fucek, 26 July, 2006
Raúl Godoy, 24 May 2013, 14 July 2006
Cándido González, 4 August 2004
Ernesto González, 25 July, 2005
Pablo Heller, 26 July 2005
Edgardo Hernan Jalil, 27 October 2015
Vanessa Jaramillo, 15 July 2006
Alejandro López, 15 July 2006

Javier Lopez, 27 July 2007
Eva Lossada, 31 October 2015
Ramiro Martínez, 27 July 2006, 23 July 2007 and 23 October 2015
Jorge Medina, 30 October 2015
Silvia Mercedes Rebón and Cristina Teijeiro, 1 and 15 July 2005
Eduardo Murúa, 21 and 26 July 2004, 8 July 2006
José Orbaiceta, 2 November 2015
Edith Oviedo, 25 July 2006
Mariano Pedrero, 7 July 2005, 13 July 2006
Julián Rebón, 16 July 2007
Fábio Resino, 28 July 2007
Diego Ruarte, 31 October 2015
Cecilia Sainz, 21 July 2005
Federico Tonarelli, 2 November 2015
Franca Venturi, 3 November 2015

INDEX

United States cooperatives: Cleveland, 149–50; Cooperative Home Care Associates (CHCA), 148; factory occupations, 111, 112–13; interlocking commercial connections, 149–50; Madison, WI support, 105; Mondragón-United Steelworkers (USW) agreement, 142–3, 146–8; New Era Windows Cooperative, 111, 115–16; New York City support, 104–5, 105; numbers and diversity, 104, 110; working-class representation, 148
Uruguay, cooperatives, 85

Venezuela: cooperative formation, 86; MINEC (Ministry of Communal Economy), 85; National Workers' Union (UNT), 83, 84–5; Social Production Enterprises (EPS), 86; Third International Solidarity Congress, 83–4; worker co-management, 83–4

wages: Argentina, 54, 67, 73, 79–80; cooperative sharing, 42, 67, 73; Cuba, 123; impact of technology, 24; minimum wage, 23; severance payments, 107, 114; US, 18, 23; wage differentials, 43, 79–80
Walzer, Michael, 89
women, 42, 67–8
work-life balance, 7
worker cooperatives: alternative to capitalism, 103–4, 155; authenticity,

35–6; authoritarian repression, 46–7; autonomy, 42, 43, 80; characteristics, 41–3; Cuba, 41; and eminent domain, 33, 97–8, 107–11; and human development, 155; need for community support, 107, 115; occupation of facilities, 48, 107; processes for creation, 107–8, 112–13; public opinion, 112; right to establish, 40; self-managed experiments, 37–8; work environment flexibility, 153; *see also* Argentine cooperative movement; Argentine cooperatives; Cuban cooperatives; Mondragón cooperative; United States cooperatives
worker participation, 39, 41, 43–4, 65–6, 67, 69, 79–80, 145, 153–4
working class: employment insecurity, 27–31, 36, 40; lack of control, 1–5; middle-class workers as, 37–9; and paternalism, 7–8; potential for rebellion, 5–8; powers of collective action, 9–13; second-class citizens, 22; subordination by technology, 24–6
The Working World, 87, 111, 115
Wright, Eric Olin, 39

Youngstown Sheet and Tube Company, 99–100

Zanón ceramic factory (FaSinPat), 63–9, 90–1